"After more than 40 [years...] best. There's nobody [better at booking guests. If there was a Hall of] Fame for producers, Randy would get in on the first ballot. The list of those he somehow convinced to come on radio shows is a who's who's of the sports world and beyond. I was lucky enough to be in front of the microphone for many of those interviews."

– **Bob Berger, former host,
One-On-One Sports/Sporting News Radio**

"In our years together I saw Randy go from green to whatever the opposite is when it comes to experience. I also saw him go from black to grey (now I'm talking hair), maybe from having to deal with us! But when it came to guest booking, I've never been with anyone better. My partner, Bob Berger, and I would marvel at his naivete when it came to his guest pursuits, and what he said he could deliver, until he actually DELIVERED and almost all of the time! What a great joy it was for us to have those conversations, thanks to Randy's passion and 'never take no for an answer approach.' He was the best!"

– **Bruce Murray, former host, One-On-One Sports/Sporting News Radio and current host, SiriusXM's NFL Radio**

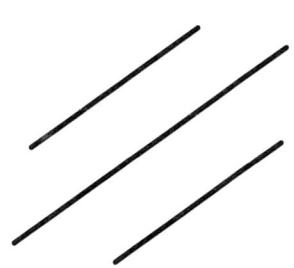

BEHIND THE GLASS
STORIES FROM A SPORTS RADIO PRODUCER

FROM STEINBRENNER TO BARKLEY TO JACK LEMMON

BY RANDY MERKIN

ECKHARTZ
PRESS

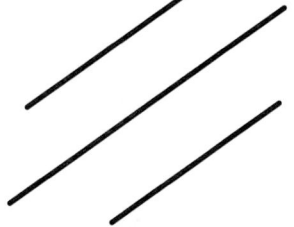

Copyright © 2021 Randy Merkin

Published in the United States by
Eckhartz Press
Chicago, Illinois

All rights reserved.

No part of this book may be used or reproduced in any manner whatsoever without written permission except in the case of brief quotations embodied in critical articles and reviews.

Cover Photo Credit: Susan Ryan Kalina Photography

ISBN: 978-1-7360774-9-8

Dedicated to my late father, Edward Merkin, who was an amazing father and taught me the work ethic that I bring every day. He was not a sports lover himself, but he raised three sons who are passionate about sports.

This book is also dedicated to my wonderful twins, Brett & Dana. I do everything with you in mind. I hope you learn from my example that hard work pays off. I want you to be the best version of yourselves.

FOREWORD

Randy Merkin has been a colleague and a friend for almost twenty years. When he approached me and asked me to write the foreword for his book, I didn't hesitate to say yes. My time with Randy was always enjoyable and I continually admired his professionalism. Randy has done and will continue to do his job with honesty and sincerity. I have no doubt that this book will be a great template of how to book guests the right way. He is one of the best in the industry and he does it with integrity and class.

Randy and I worked side by side for years when I hosted a two-hour radio show for Sporting News Radio. Randy's attention to detail was amazing. He never left any stone unturned. No matter who I was interviewing, I was prepared for the interview. Randy made my job easier, but he also made it fun. Sometimes doing sports radio can be a grind, but Randy knew when to pull back or when to push me. He also had no fear. He woke me up after a crazy week at the Super Bowl to tape an interview with Tony Dungy. I knew Randy wouldn't have called unless it was important.

What sets Randy apart is his character. He was always concerned about me as a person and how I was doing. I also really enjoyed my time with Randy when we weren't talking about the shows or business. Even after we worked together, I would get a text from Randy every Thanksgiving wishing me a happy holiday. That goes a long way! Sometimes people only reach out to you when they need something from you, but that's not Randy. For example, I received a text from Randy on my 70th birthday. It meant the world to me that he took the time to reach out! I have been in the sports media industry for many years and I have worked with a lot of people. I am so thrilled that I had the opportunity to work with a pro like Randy Merkin. I will always cherish our times together and I look forward to reading Randy's many great guest-booking stories.

While we cherish champions in the world of sports, we cheer louder for champions in the game of life. Character, integrity and honesty matter. That sums up Randy Merkin.

– James "JB" Brown, Host of *NFL Today* on CBS
and *Inside the NFL* on Showtime

TABLE OF CONTENTS

BASEBALL

George Steinbrenner #1 2
Paul Molitor, Hank Aaron and Tony Gwynn 4
Pete Rose...............................6
Jose Canseco.........................8
Goose Gossage......................9
Rick Ankiel..........................10
Josh Hamilton 11
Bruce Bochy 13
Ryne Sandberg and Bruce Sutter.......................14
Ernie Banks 15
Lou Piniella 16
Theo Epstein.......................18
John Smoltz 19
Ryne Sandberg 20
Cooperstown......................22
Cal Ripken 24
George Steinbrenner #2 25
Torii Hunter 26

NBA BASKETBALL

Kobe Bryant.......................30
Dwyane Wade 31
Dikembe Mutombo.............33
Scottie Pippen 34
Michael Jordan...................35

Phil Jackson........................37
Charles Barkley #1...............39
Shaquille O'Neal 41
Jerry Krause........................43
Charles Barkley #2...............45

COLLEGE BASKETBALL

Rick Pitino..........................50
Jim Boeheim.......................51
John Calipari......................52
Jim Calhoun 53
Bo Ryan..............................54
Rick Majerus and Al Maguire...........................56

NFL FOOTBALL

Peyton Manning 70
Bill Parcells and Drew Bledsoe 71
Bill Walsh...........................72
Harry Carson 73
Terry Bradshaw...................75
Tony Dungy 76
John and Jim Harbaugh 78
Terrell Owens.....................80
Mike Ditka.........................81
Mike Singletary...................84
Bill Parcells 85

TABLE OF CONTENTS (CONT.)

NFL Draft 87
Troy Aikman 89
John Elway..............................90
Andy Reid................................92
Kurt Warner 93
Bart Starr 94
Brandon Marshall................96
Tim Dwight and
Jeff Garcia 97
Johnny Unitas 98

COLLEGE FOOTBALL

Jim Harbaugh 102
John David Washington 103
Dabo Sweeny 104
Tim Tebow............................105
AJ McCarron........................106

GOLF

Tom Watson 110
Dustin Johnson....................111
Brooks Koepka.....................112
Rocco Mediate 113
Greg Norman &
Chris Evert...........................114
Justin Leonard.....................115
Scott Dunlap 116
Johnny Miller.......................118
Jack Nicklaus.......................119
2 Holes in One 121

BOXING, HOCKEY, HORSES & TENNIS

John McEnroe......................126
Wayne Gretzky....................128
Floyd Mayweather 130
Mike Eruzione and
Al Michaels..........................131
The Kentucky Derby 132
Mike Tyson..........................133
Evander Holyfield................135

MEDIA

Jim Nantz.............................138
Dick Enberg.........................139
Tom Brokaw 141
Al Michaels..........................142
Big Cat..................................143

CELEBRITIES

Eddie Vedder 146
Donny Osmond 147
Jack Lemmon 148
Grandpa Munster 150
Bill Murray 151
Kenny Kraemer....................153
Henry Winkler.....................153
Snoop Dog............................155
President Obama 156
Meeting Waddle & Silvy 157

BASEBALL

George Steinbrenner #1

Booking guests for radio shows used to be a lot different. There were no cell phones or even agents to help. Everything was set up through public relations staff or by calling hotels directly to find desired guests.

It was the winter of 1995 and I was a producer for the national radio show, "Mariotti and Gentzkow." I had been working at One-On-One Sports, a national sports radio network, for about eight months and I had learned during that time that I couldn't settle, but rather, should always strive for the big-name guest. I had to book the guest who would make a difference to the listener and keep them tuned in. So, I wrote down a list of guests I wanted to book during March and April. At the top of that list was *The Boss*, George Steinbrenner. He was the untouchable guest. He was already the most famous sports team owner around before Larry David played him on Seinfeld. Then he became even bigger. Booking George Steinbrenner wasn't going to be easy since I knew that I was unlikely to get help from the Yankees PR staff. Mr. Steinbrenner always had many requests from the local New York media, so why would he take mine to speak to a national audience?

I had to be resourceful. In my Spring Training Media Guide, The Yankees listed an office number for Mr. Steinbrenner. During the first week of Spring Training, I called his direct line at 10am eastern time and his secretary answered. She had a thick New York accent. I was very polite and asked her if it was at all possible to set up an interview with Mr. Steinbrenner. (I always addressed him as *Mr. Steinbrenner* to show respect. It's the same with coaches- even if they are not currently coaching, I address them as "Coach".) As a guest booker, you can usually detect right away if there is a chance of success and during this conversation, I knew there was not. She said, "Randy, Mr. Steinbrenner does not do radio interviews." I assured her that I was just looking for five minutes of his time. She again refused so I told her I would keep calling every day until he said yes. I kept my promise and called every day and she kept hers and always said no.

One night, I was in my one-bedroom efficiency in Evanston, looking through the Spring Training Media Guide and saw a "home" hotel listed for the Yankees. While I figured that there was no way that Mr. Steinbrenner would stay there, it was worth a shot. I called the hotel at 11:30 pm eastern time. I thought that if he didn't answer after the first ring, I would hang up. I anxiously asked for his room and the operator rang me right through. I have to admit that I was nervous. He answered on the first ring and sounded wide awake. I said, "Mr. Steinbrenner, Sir, it's Randy with One-On-One Sports. How are you doing?" He answered, "Fine, young man. Do you have any idea what time it is?" Of course I did but I played dumb and told him I thought it was only 10:30pm. I apologized and wished him a good night. He said, "Wait a minute. What did you need?" I told him that I had been trying all spring to get him on our network for a radio interview. He said, "I don't do radio interviews." I told him that I understood and then he said, "Wait a minute. You call me tomorrow at 10am eastern and tell my secretary that you are the rude young man who woke me up. Then I will do the interview." I was stunned, thanked him, and hung up. The rest of the night I barely slept in anticipation of what could happen the following day.

The next morning at 10am eastern, I called Mr. Steinbrenner's office. His secretary answered. I greeted her, "Good morning, it's Randy with One-On-One Sports. Can I speak with Mr. Steinbrenner?" She said emphatically, "Randy, he doesn't do radio interviews." I asked her to tell him that it's the rude young man who woke him up last night. She seemed shocked, so I repeated my request. No more than thirty seconds later, Mr. Steinbrenner picked up the phone with great energy and said,

"Ok, let's go." I put him on the air with Mark Gentzkow and Jay Mariotti and they spoke for about twenty minutes. At the end of the interview, he told the guys, "You have one persistent producer. He has been calling every day to get me on your show and now I am on your show. Good job, young man!" I picked up the phone after the interview to thank Mr. Steinbrenner and he said, "Good work, happy to do it!" I felt a huge sense of accomplishment that day.

Paul Molitor, Hank Aaron, and Tony Gwynn

I loved doing roundtable discussions because they were a way to take a different avenue in order to provide great content to the listeners. I heard a pitching roundtable on ESPN Radio with Don Sutton and Phil Niekro, and it was fantastic, so I decided to follow that model and create a hitters roundtable, and I aimed big. I reached out to a bunch of teams to gauge interest from their star players. After a couple of weeks, I settled on three players - Wade Boggs (Tampa Bay), Paul Molitor (Minnesota) and Tony Gwynn (San Diego). The challenge was to find a time that worked with all of their schedules. I started working on this at the beginning of Spring Training. Finally, we settled on July 4th at 12pm.

I remember that day well. I came in early to make sure everything was all set. (This was back in 1999 and we were taping on reel-to-reel and I used a DAT, Digital Audio Tape, as a backup.) I had confirmed with all three players the day before, so I was hoping that they would all "show up." I was down in production when I received a call from the Tampa Bay Devil Rays. Wade Boggs was out! He sincerely apologized, but he had to cancel. Needless to say, I wasn't happy. Bob and Bruce reassured me to not worry because Tony Gwynn and Paul Molitor would still be outstanding. However, I was really upset because I was hoping to have three hall-of-fame hitters together and now I only had two.

I started looking at teams on the road. Were there any great hitters playing later in the day that I could try on the fly? Dave Parker, The Cobra, was the A's hitting coach. I tried calling him in the hotel, but he didn't answer. Then I aimed even bigger. What about Willie Mays or Hank Aaron? I had a fairly good relationship with Hank Aaron. I had called him at home a couple of times over the previous years and he was always great. So, I called his home number and his wife informed me that he was at the park because the Braves had a 1pm game. It was now around 11:25 and we were taping in thirty-five minutes. I called Turner Field and asked for Hank Aaron's office. On the fourth ring, he answered, and I was shocked. I said, "Mr. Aaron, I know this is a crazy request but I'm about to tape a hitters roundtable in thirty minutes with Tony Gwynn and Paul Molitor. Would you have any interest in being involved?" He asked how long of a time commitment this would entail and I told him around thirty minutes. He asked where he would have to go, and I told him that he could do it from his office. He said, "That sounds like fun. I will do it!" I was beyond excited! I asked for the best phone number to call him, and he gave me his direct line. Before I hung up, he asked me, "Randy, do you know how lucky you are? Your call came on my assistant's line, and I rarely answer her phone!"

It was now time for the roundtable. Tony Gwynn called in right on time. I thanked him for his time and told him that Wade Boggs had to cancel, but I went to our bench to fill his spot. He said, "Oh yeah, who did you get? When I said, "Hank Aaron," he paused for a second and then started laughing and said, "You got some fucking bench!" Paul Molitor called in next. I also informed him of the change, and he was thrilled. Finally, I called Hank Aaron, who seemed very appreciative that we included him. Bob and Bruce told the guys that this roundtable is all about them and they should feel free to jump in and even take over the conversation if they wanted. Five minutes in, Hank Aaron jumped in and asked Bob and Bruce if he could ask Tony and Paul a specific question about their two-strike approach. For the next fifteen minutes, it was just the three of them talking. It was fantastic! It was one of the most memorable interviews I ever arranged. Seventeen years later, Hank Aaron agreed to do an interview with my son for a school project. What a great guy!

Pete Rose

I have always had great success booking Pete Rose. I'm not sure why, but it may be due to his relationship with Tom Waddle. Pete was in town for a card show and I figured it was a good time to do an in-person show with him. We worked out the details with his agency and he was all set to be our *Lunch with a Legend* guest on a Monday at noon. (*Lunch with a Legend* was a series we did with high-profile athletes or celebrities at Morton's Steakhouse.) I arranged for Pete to arrive around 12pm to go on the air at 1pm with Carmen, Jurko and Tom Waddle. I got a call at around 10:45 am from Pete's guy saying, "Hey, Pete says he wants to come over early. We should be there by 11." Well, I was glad that he was excited to get started, but I was a little nervous. What was I going to do with Pete Rose for two hours? I would have him do a brief "meet and greet" with some clients and sign some baseballs, but that would only take thirty minutes tops.

Pete arrived at 11am and waddled up the stairs into a special room we had set up for him. I introduced myself and our marketing director, Elena Angelos, introduced herself. Pete sat down and signed all the baseballs. He was very accommodating. That whole process probably took fifteen minutes, so it was now 11:15 and clients had not yet arrived. While I went to get Pete something to drink, it hit me that I had one of the top twenty baseball players right there, sitting next to me! I had to take advantage of this situation. So, for the next hour, Pete regaled me and my fellow producer, JR Straus, with many great stories. For example, I heard about his first All-Star Game when his locker was between Willie Mays and Hank Aaron. I was excited to tell him about one of my favorite Cub moments when he hit a line-drive off of Lee Smith's back and Larry Bowa made the catch to end the game. At that moment, Harry Caray said, "The good Lord wants the Cubs to win!" Pete Rose entertained us with story after story after story. Each was better than the last, but they were all full of swear words, which concerned me, since he would soon be on live radio.

Next, we did the meet and greet with the clients and then it was time for Pete to go on the air. I put my arm around him and said, "Pete, I loved our time together, but you are about to go live on the radio. You have to do me a favor and not swear, ok?" He looked at me and joked, "You f****** got it, Randy." Well, he did an entire hour of great radio in front of a sold-out crowd and only swore once! After the show, he came up to me with this big grin on his face. "How did I f****** do, Rand?" he asked. "You were great, Pete!" I replied, and I meant it.

Pete jumped into the car with "Limo Bill," the driver we use, to head to the airport. Waddle went back to the studio to do his show. He told Silvy how great the interview was and how great Pete smelled - yes, smelled! Little did we know that Pete was listening in the car. He texted me and asked for Waddle's address and, while I thought it was odd, I also thought maybe he wanted to send him a thank-you note. I gave Waddle a heads up. About a month later, Waddle received a package with a gigantic bottle of cologne and a note that read, "Tom, now you can smell like a man! All the best, *The Hit King* Pete Rose." It remains one of Tom's most prized possessions. I still can't believe I spent an entire hour listening to baseball stories from *The Hit King*!

Jose Canseco

Jose Canseco was a polarizing player. In his prime, he was one of the best. However, after he finished his career, we learned he did most of it while on steroids. Years after he was done, shockingly, he became the voice of reason on the topic. He was the guy who came clean first and he wrote a book in which he exposed other players and informed us about how the steroid system worked. When steroid news broke, you went to Jose Canseco for confirmation.

Jose was always a little difficult to deal with. He was a different kind of personality. I had tried to book him in the past, but without great success. On May 7, 2009, Manny Ramirez got pinched for steroids. Possibly the best right-handed hitter of his time was going away for a while. I remember where I was when it happened. I had the day off from work and was in the Neiman Marcus parking lot at Northbrook Court. I was about to go in and buy my wife a birthday gift when Adam Delevitt, our Program Director, called me and said, "Merk, we have to cancel Bulls Guard Lyndsey Hunter. Manny Ramirez was just suspended." I responded, "No problem. Do you want me to try anyone?" Adam asked who I was thinking about. I told him to give me a minute. I looked up Canseco's cell and called him. He answered right away. I said, "Jose, it's Randy with ESPN 1000. Did you hear that Manny was suspended for fifty games?" Of course, he did. I asked, "Can you come on ESPN 1000 and talk about it?" When he agreed to, I said, "Great, I have to call you back from another number to make sure you are Jose Canseco, the voice of the people." He responded, "The one and only!" He came on with Waddle and Silvy and was fantastic.

Fast forward to Jan 10, 2011. Mark McGwire, who was Jose Canseco's teammate with the A's for many years, conducted an interview in which he admitted to steroid use. In that interview he said Jose Canseco never injected him with steroids. Well, the next morning I was producing *Waddle and Silvy*. Jonathan Hood was filling in for Tom Waddle. I called Jose Canseco around 9:30 and asked him if he had watched the Mark McGwire interview. He responded, "I did. Lies, nothing but lies!" I told him we needed him on ESPN 1000. He said, "Sure." I put him on right away with Silvy and J. Hood. If I remember correctly, *Sportscenter* went live to the interview. It was compelling stuff. He called out McGwire for not telling the truth in claiming that Jose had never injected him. Jose said that he had injected him many times. He was on for about fourteen minutes. When he was done, I thanked him for coming on and he said that it was no problem.

When the interview was done, the next step was to transcribe it and send it out to as many outlets as possible. This was long before Twitter was as popular as it was today. We sent the transcriptions and audio out all across the country. The interview was so powerful that it forced Mark McGwire to do another interview, this time with *Baseball Tonight*, to refute what Jose Canseco had said. In all my time booking guests, that was a first! That night on the 6 and 10 pm *Sportscenter* shows, their lead was a four-minute clip from the interview with Silvy and J. Hood. It is really cool to reflect on that experience. It was a huge story and I'm proud that we had a small part in advancing it.

Goose Gossage

Goose Gossage is as old school as they come. He is a Hall of Famer who never holds back with his opinions. Around three years ago, he went off on how the game was played. It made huge news, so I texted him and asked him to come on with Waddle and Silvy. He got back to me that afternoon and agreed to do the interview. He was great with the guys and they ended up using one of his cuts for their open. Recently there was an incident in baseball where Fernando Tatis swung at a 3-0 pitch with the bases loaded and a 4-run lead. The baseball world went nuts. I decided to get the opinion of some of the old-school baseball legends. I texted George Brett, Fergie Jenkins, Bruce Bochy, Pete Rose, and Goose Gossage.

I was hoping to get a comment from them that I could read on the air, but none of them responded.

When I was driving home, Goose Gossage called me. I was hesitant to answer because I didn't know how he would respond to my text. I decided to answer. He said, "Rand, it's Goose."

"Hey Goose."

"Tell me about this Tatis play."

I told him all about it and for the next twenty minutes I listened to Goose go off on today's game. He didn't hold back about anyone. His thoughts certainly were not aligned with the way today's baseball minds think, but it's how he believed the game should be played. I said, "Goose, I love your passion. I will call you tomorrow and we can record something."

"No because then they will all come after me again for being the old guy in the room."

"Since when do you care about that?"

"Ok call me tomorrow but I have friends coming in." Then he continued on his rant. I told him again, five minutes later, I would call him tomorrow. He said, "No - they will just call me old. But if I'm free, I will answer." Well, I tried a few times the next day and he never answered. Hopefully someday he will!

Rick Ankiel

Rick Ankiel is the one that got away. What an amazing story! At one time, Rick was one of the bright young arms in the MLB. Then he couldn't find the plate. Most people thought his career was over, however, he went back to the minors and learned how to hit. Then the Cardinals called him up. His first game up was great and he had the game-winning RBI. His was the story of MLB and everyone was trying to book him.

The old guest-booker trick was that when a player is called and they are playing at the home ballpark, they most likely are staying at a hotel near the park. I followed that theory and called the main hotels in St. Louis and found him! I called the hotel without asking Waddle and Silvy if they were interested and hoped they would be. We had just spent the last two days at Bears camp, and I had only worked with the guys for just over a month. I still felt like I could convince them if Rick was available. Well, Rick answered right away, and I was psyched! I congratulated him and asked if he might have a few minutes for us. He said, "Yes, but make it quick!" I told him that we were going to break and asked if I could call back in ten minutes. He told me, "Yes, but no later."

I went in the studio at the break and told the guys. Silvy was lukewarm on the idea and Waddle had little interest. Waddle asked, "Why don't you have Chet (Coppock) tape him?" To this day, it bugs me that I didn't make them do the interview. I went and sought out Chet. He, of course, was overjoyed to do the interview, but he said, "Merk give me 30 minutes to do some research." I said, "Chet, you have five." We were already at twenty minutes since I called Rick. By the time Chet got ready, it was now thirty minutes. I called the hotel, but Rick didn't answer. I was upset that I missed my chance! It's crazy that sometimes I remember the ones who got away more than the great ones that I booked!

Josh Hamilton

Josh Hamilton was one talented baseball player who had a real checkered past with drugs. It was very sad because he could have been one of the greats. In 2008, Josh Hamilton was a star player for the Texas Rangers. He was having a fantastic season and everyone was looking forward to seeing him compete in the Home Run Derby. All-Star games were always a fun time for me since you could usually reach star MLB players that you had no chance of booking during the season.

On that particular Monday, Josh Hamilton was on my list of

potential guests along with Tim Lincecum and Joe Mauer. I called Josh's room around 11 am. He answered, but I could tell he was a little out of it. I asked if he might have a few minutes to join us. He said, "Bro, I didn't get in till late. I need to sleep. Can we do this the same time tomorrow?" I said, "Of course." When an athlete tells you that, in the back of your mind you always think there is no way they will remember 24 hours later. I was also hoping he didn't go nuts that night in the Home Run Derby, or the media would all want to talk to him.

Nothing beats a Home Run Derby in Yankee Stadium. That night Josh Hamilton put on a show. Like Babe Ruth back in the day, he was hitting home run after home run and each seemed to go further than the one before. With each passing home run, I kept thinking, there is no way Josh Hamilton will be listed tomorrow. Everyone is going to want to book him. I did have one thing in my favor. I had done some research on Josh and read a great story in *Sports Illustrated*. It said that on every road trip, Josh's father-in-law stayed at the room next to him - almost acting as a chaperone.

The next morning, I called Josh's room around 10:50 to just remind him about the interview. Just as I suspected, he was no longer listed! We had promoted that he was coming on at 11. Now he wasn't listed. I had no cell on Josh, but I did have his father-in-law's name. I called the hotel and asked for his room. They rang it and he answered on the first ring. I explained to him the situation and he told me to hold on, he went across the hall, and he knocked on Josh's door. He said, "Hey, do you have an interview to do at 11?" He said, "Oh you're right, I do." He continued, "Give him my cell." I called him ten minutes later and he was great! We played some highlights for him. I'm pretty sure he did the interview from the bathroom. Anyways, Josh had maybe the most historic night in Home Run Derby history and the following day he was on with Waddle and Silvy. It was amazing!

By the way, on Monday I did reach Tim Lincecum and Joe

Mauer. Tim was happy to come on. Joe said to try him on Tuesday and then called the Twins PR to complain. I got an earful that day from the Twins PR person, but it was all worth it!

Bruce Bochy

Bruce Bochy is one of the most underrated managers of his time and a heck of a nice guy. He had an amazing run with the Giants. I had Bruce Bochy's cell phone number for years. However, when he went to the Giants, the number changed. I was able to get his new cell and planned on using it if the Giants won the World Series. Well, the Giants won their first of three World Series in five years.

At that time, I was producing Waddle and Silvy. The night they won, I sent Bochy a text asking if there was any chance, he could join us the next day. There was no response. I sent that text because they were on the west coast and I didn't think he would be up at 7am. The show progressed the next day with Waddle and Silvy and I hadn't heard a word from Bruce. I sent him another text and still didn't get a response. Back then Waddle and Silvy were on from 9-12 and then we aired the *Dan Patrick Show*. My final window was 11:50, so I tried calling him at 11:30 and it went right to voicemail. I figured he must have been sleeping. I tried one more time as we were coming back from our final break. Bruce answered and said, "Hey ya, Randy. I saw your text. I was going to call you later today. Is that ok?" I said, "Actually, Bruce, can we do it this second?" He laughed and said, "Sure, I'm just sitting here in my office with my coaches." I typed it on the screen to Waddle and Silvy and said, "Go to Bruce Bochy now!" They did a great job and went right to him. We only had six minutes with him, but it was perfect. As a guest booker there is nothing better than getting the big name the day after a major title. It's another example of persistence paying off, while not being obnoxious.

Ryne Sandberg and Bruce Sutter

Growing up, my favorite Cub was Jose Cardenal. That was until the Cubs traded for Ryne Sandberg. I loved everything about Ryne's game and now I was booking Ryne on a regular basis. I will detail those bookings in another story. However, I had the idea on June 23, 2008 to book Ryne and Bruce Sutter to celebrate Ryne's most famous game as a Cub. If you don't remember it, Ryne hit two homeruns in the 9th and 10th off Bruce Sutter. No one did that! I bet Bruce Sutter didn't give up more than five homeruns in a single season.

I worked with Ryne's PR firm and set him up for Waddle and Silvy. However, I was having issues getting in touch with Bruce Sutter. Then I received an email from the network saying that if anyone wanted to interview Bruce Sutter, he was available if you promoted the product he was pitching. I couldn't believe my luck. I reached out to his contact and explained what I wanted to do. She said she would ask Bruce. He said he would love to be a part of it. They both joined Waddle and Silvy the next day and the interview was outstanding! We came out of the break with the two home runs called by Bob Costas. Bruce was a great sport about the whole thing. Our plan was to do one long segment with both guys and then bring Ryne back to talk some general baseball in the next segment. One thing about Ryne... since his playing days were done, he became a much better interview and always gave an honest answer. I told Waddle and Silvy the one question we had to ask is if Sammy Sosa is a Hall of Famer. If we got the answer we were looking for, I knew it would go viral. Well, Silvy asked him, "Ryne, does Sammy Sosa belong in the Hall?" Ryne responded without hesitation, "NO!" He said, "Part of making the Hall is having integrity and doing things without cheating!" He doubled down with his next answer. Back in the day, Twitter wasn't a big thing. What I would do is either transcribe the interview myself or have my interns transcribe it. As soon as we transcribed Ryne's answers, I sent it to all the papers.

The following day, on the back of the *Sun Times* newspaper, in big bold letters it said, "Ryne Sandberg says no Hall of Fame for Sammy Sosa." Needless to say, other outlets picked it up as well. I was proud of what we had accomplished and that we did it with my favorite Cub!

Ernie Banks

What Cub fan doesn't idolize Ernie Banks? He set the standard for greatness. Well, when I started at ESPN, it was a goal of mine to have Ernie come in studio. I worked with his PR people and set it up to have him come in studio with Waddle and Silvy for 11 am on a Wednesday. I was psyched! I usually don't do this, but I decided to bring in a baseball for Ernie to sign.

Well, the day he was scheduled to come in I get a call around 9:15. It was Ernie. He said, "Randy, what's your address?" I gave it to him. He said, "Oh, I don't live far from there. I'm on my way over."

"Wait Ernie, you aren't scheduled to come on until 11."

"I want to come over and hang out."

Sure enough by 9:40am, Ernie was sitting in the producer studio with myself. He was intrigued about how a radio show worked. Finally, the time came for him to go on with Waddle and Silvy. He was very friendly and gave great answers during the first segment. We planned to keep him for two segments, so I went into the studio at the break to see if Ernie needed anything. As I opened the door, I heard him say to Waddle, "Tom, did your wife breastfeed your children?" I wanted to turn around and walk out, but I also wanted to hear the rest of this conversation. Like the true pro Tom is, he answered Ernie seriously and said she did for the first three children, but by the fourth, she was too tired. I then jumped and asked Ernie if he needed anything. He responded and said, "Randy, are you married?" I said,

"Yes."

"How is your wife?"

"Great!"

We finished up the second segment. Ernie came back in the producer studio to say goodbye. Our GM, John Cravens, was a huge fan of Ernie's. He came in to say hi and take a picture with Ernie. After the segment was done, I walked Ernie out. Half an hour later, I was walking to the bathroom and, as I walked by John's office, I saw Ernie sitting in his office! I said, "Ernie, what are you still doing here?"

"I want that light-up Budweiser sign that Mr. Cravens has. What's your price, John?"

"Come on, Ernie, John has to do some work." As I was walking him out, Ernie said he wanted to come back. I said, "Next time Ernie, call your friends Willie and Hank."

"No problem!"

A side story about Ernie... Years before, I attended a Sox/Yankees game with Bob Berger and Bruce Murray. They had great seats. As we got to our seats, there were two people sitting there. Bob, without hesitation, in a polite manner, said, "Excuse me, can you please move? You're in our seats." The two gentlemen got up and moved two rows behind us. I said, "Berger, do you know who you just kicked out of our seats?"

"No. Who?"

"Ernie Banks and Gale Sayers! What were you thinking?"

Lou Piniella

Sweet Lou Piniella was one of my favorite managers that the Cubs have ever employed. Charismatic and always full of enthusiasm is the best way to describe Lou. It was a big deal when he took over the helm for the Cubs. I had a cell and home number for Lou in Tampa. During the year, Lou was pretty much off-limits. His first year with the Cubs, he shocked everyone and took them to the playoffs. Unfortunately, they got swept by the Diamondbacks. Well,

I thought having Lou on would be a great way to recap the season. I waited two days after the season was over to call his home in Tampa on a Wednesday night and he answered and was very friendly. I congratulated him on a great season, and, in typical Lou fashion, he said "Gee, thanks. What's up?"

"Do you possibly have time tomorrow to join Waddle and Silvy?"

He asked what time.

"How about 11 am eastern time?"

He said that was great.

So, the next day I called Lou at 11. He was outstanding with the guys. Four minutes into the interview I got a call on the hotline from our baseball insider, Bruce Levine, informing me that the Cubs PR were not pleased that I called Lou at home. I was kind of surprised by that, considering the season was over. I told Bruce that I was just doing my job and that Lou is a grown man and agreed to do the interview. The best part of the interview was Silvy asking Lou if he was staying with the Cubs. The Yankees were looking for a new manager and rumor had it that Lou was in the running. He shot that rumor down on the air and it made news all across Chicago.

The Following year, the Cubs were the number one seed in the playoffs and again got swept, this time by the Dodgers. I decided to call Lou at home once again. I waited two days to let him get settled. Once again, he was very friendly and remembered me from last year. He said he would be happy to come on. So, the next morning Lou joined Waddle and Silvy. Again, around four minutes into the interview, I got a call from Bruce saying the Cubs PR was not happy with me. I told Bruce I was doing my job, but this would be the last year that I would call Lou while he was the manager of the Cubs. As always, he was great, a willing participant and an entertaining interview. A couple of years after he left the Cubs job, I put him on with Waddle and Silvy. I picked up the phone before he went on and told him, "Hey, Silvy just got engaged. You have to give him crap!" He said, "Oh, ok. You said Silvy got engaged?" Silvy welcomed Lou and without missing a beat, Lou congratulated Silvy on his engagement. I think Silvy was very surprised. It was a cool moment. I always loved booking Lou. He was a great character of the game.

Theo Epstein

Alex Rodriguez, AKA Arod, was the big fish to get in 2004. It was coming down between the two hated rivals the Yanks and the Red Sox. I remember it well. It was a Saturday afternoon when we got the word that Arod was signing with the Yanks. What a huge story to land in our laps on Saturday afternoon! This is what you live for as a producer. No one was off-limits. I wish I had a phone number for Arod, but no go. First up was Theo Epstein, the man who built the Boston Red Sox into a dynasty.

Back in 2004, texting still wasn't that popular, so I called Theo on his cell phone. He answered right away and was cordial. I asked him to come on to talk about Arod signing with the Yankees. He said, "Randy, we never talk about our opponents' moves and second of all, what are you thinking, man?" I was confused. I said, "What are you talking about, Theo?"

"Come on, man. You can't call me on a holiday."

I responded in a confused manner, "Valentine's Day?"

"Yes, and thanks for calling." And then he hung up.

One down, I still had two more to go. Next up was the Red Sox Manager, Tito Francona. Tito is the best. I called him at home, and he was cordial as well. He thought it was cool having Arod in the division. I asked if he could come on and he said, "Randy, I would love to, but it's my daughter's birthday party and I promised her no work today." I couldn't argue with that. He said, "Feel free to call me another time." My last big fish was Curt Schilling. Say what you want about Curt's post-baseball career, but when he was playing, he was a great interview and always a willing participant. I called him at home and was very friendly. I think I broke the news to him about Arod. He yelled to his wife, "The Yanks got Arod!" I said, "Hey, would you be able to join us for a few minutes?" He said, "Absolutely." I put him on with Bob and Bruce. He was outstanding and welcomed the challenge of facing Arod. I thought afterwards, "What a grind!" One big story and one big guest to react! That's what it's all about!

John Smoltz

John Smoltz is one of my favorite guests to book. I will argue with anyone that John Smoltz is a top-five interview in Sports Radio. Back when I was working at One-On-One Sports/Sporting News Radio, he was a regular with us. I had him on at least three times each season.

In 2000, John Smoltz underwent Tommy John Surgery. I reached out to our reporter who covered the Braves. I said, "Can you ask John if he would consider doing a weekly with us during the entire season?" He asked John and his response was, "Absolutely!" He didn't ask for a weekly payment, but rather that we make a donation to his foundation, which we happily did.

I didn't know what to expect from John. I figured he would be doing a lot of rehab and would probably miss many weekends. Nothing could be further from the truth. He was outstanding! Not only did he call in every weekend, but he usually checked in with me on Friday to set up a time. Then when he called in on Saturday or Sunday, he would give me a few topics that he wanted to address. I'm telling you, he's the best. The following April, we were at the Final Four in Atlanta. We were entering the game and I saw John walking in with his family. I sprinted over to say hello. I think I startled him, but not surprisingly, he was cordial and spoke to me for a few minutes. All in all, the season worked out great.

My second John Smoltz story still troubles me to this day. As I mentioned, we had a great relationship with John. He was playing at Michael Jordan's tourney in the Bahamas. I called him in the hotel, and he said he would be happy to come on for five minutes. I put him with Doug Russell the day after the Braves' long time pitching coach, Leo Mazzone, had retired. He had been with Smoltz, Maddux, and Glavine for years. I had the bright idea to call Leo and surprise John by putting them on together. Of course, Leo was happy to do it. Doug set it up perfectly. He said, "How much will you miss Leo Mazzone?" John responded, "Well, not that much because veteran pitchers like myself, Mad Dog and Glavine basically know what to do." I was waving my arms to Doug to not put him on, but it was too late! Doug said, "Let's welcome in your former pitching coach." Leo right away said, "John, you aren't going to miss me?" Doug was able to salvage the interview and make a joke of it, but needless to say, after the interview John was not happy. I couldn't apologize enough. Eventually he got past it, but I learned my lesson about surprises on the air.

Ryne Sandberg

Every once in a while, even in the position I'm in, I am still a fan. Growing up, Ryne Sandberg was my favorite player. I had many great memories with Ryne through the years and a few stand out. The first one was actually over the phone. The Cubs were struggling and there was a good chance they were going to replace their manager. Once the Cubs fired their manager through the process of hiring their new manager, Ryne was great to Waddle and Silvy. At the time, Ryne was a manager in the Cubs' minor league system and, not only did he always come on our station, but he was honest that he wanted to be the next Cubs manager. The Cubs finally made a decision, but it wasn't Ryno. They went with Mike Quade and a lot of Cub fans weren't happy. Ryno was the guy to get on the air. I remember I texted him and called him, but he didn't respond. Then a half hour later, I saw the hotline ringing and it was Ryne's number. He said, "Hey, I saw you guys called me. You need me?" He came on and was great since he really poured out his feelings. It was fantastic radio! I truly believe the main reason he called back is because he trusted Waddle and Silvy and the relationship we had built with Ryne over the years.

The second memory took place in 2016. The Cubs were on the cusp of clinching the division. I came up with the idea of doing a show from St. Louis where the Cubs were hopefully going to clinch. Then we brainstormed and came up with a brilliant idea and decided to include Ryne Sandberg in it. We qualified 20 listeners and brought them from Chicago to St. Louis on a bus. They stayed overnight at a nice hotel and the next day they went to the Cubs vs Cardinals afternoon game and sat in a luxury box with Ryne Sandberg and his wife. David Kaplan and I traveled down a day earlier and did our shows from ESPN St. Louis. The Cubs/Cards was an afternoon game and, if the Cubs won, they clinched a tie for the division.

The game started at 1pm, and Kap was on until 2pm. I was not happy since I wanted to be there right at the start to hang out with Ryne. Kap and I wrapped up the show and sprinted to the new Cardinal stadium. We arrived in the 4th inning. I still remember walking into the box and seeing Ryno sitting there with his wife talking to some fans. I usually don't become a fan, but for a minute I did! I went up to Ryne, introduced myself and told him I was the person dealing with his agent to set his event up. He said he was very happy with how it was handled. Then I just peppered him with questions. I told him the reason my son wears #23 is because of him and Michael Jordan. A couple minutes later, I left him alone, but not until I took a picture with Ryne. Each time he was in studio, I took a picture. Later that day, I was thinking back to what had transpired and I thought, "I just watched the Cubs clinch the division with my boyhood idol!" Not a bad day.

Cooperstown

For any baseball fan, Cooperstown is heaven. In the summer of 2019 I had the opportunity to go there for a tournament with my son and his travel baseball team from Deerfield. I have to admit, a couple of weeks before, I was dreading going. The team wasn't playing well, and we had a 13-hour car ride ahead of us. We went with one of Brett's teammates, Josh, and his dad, Scott Peterman, and it was actually an easy trip. Once we arrived to drop the kids off at their dorm, I saw why everyone loves this trip. It was baseball Nirvana! The fields were immaculate and there was a different theme for each. I knew right then that this would be an amazing trip for Brett and me. They played two games for three straight days and then there were playoffs. From the first game on, it was an amazing experience. Brett's team played great! They almost beat one of the best teams from California, but they ended up tying. Brett was playing pretty well and seeing his face after each game made the whole trip worthwhile. After our first game, we went to the Cooperstown Museum. It was very cool to walk around the hallowed grounds and point out to Brett and his friends all the amazing things on display.

Then I got a text around 11:30pm, which was after our 4th game. It was from Brett and he said, "Dad, I'm starting tomorrow morning."

"Great. You know what tomorrow is, right?"

"Grandpa's birthday."

The next morning I saw him before the start of the game, and I told him to go out and just have fun. No pressure! Well, he had a great time as he pitched the game of his life. He gave up a run in the first inning, but then settled in. The games were 6 innings long. He got through 4 innings with a 7-3 lead. Since that's the most number of innings anyone in his league had pitched, I figured he was done. Nope. He came out for the 5th. My heart was beating so fast. That was the best inning he pitched yet. Then came the bottom of the

5th. The one thing Brett wanted was a homerun at Cooperstown, but he just missed it. The ball had the distance, but just pulled foul! He ended up getting a double and driving in two runs. I could now breathe. There is no way the coach, Shane Mulhern, would bring him out for the 6th. Then one of the other dads, Pete Jones, sat down next me and said, "Merk is going out for the complete game. I just heard Shane ask if he had one more and Brett said yes. In the back of my mind I was thinking, "Oh my - a complete game at Cooperstown. That would be unreal." And he did it! The last inning went 1-2-3! After the game, I waited for him outside. He came out with the biggest grin on his face. I had tears in my eyes for two reasons. I was so proud of him and I couldn't wait to call my dad and tell him what a great game his grandson had.

I walked up the big hill at Cooperstown and called my dad. I said, "Hey Dad, happy birthday! You are not going to believe what Brett just did. He threw a complete game at Cooperstown and just missed a homerun."

"Mom says you don't remember when we took you to the Hall of Fame?"

"Dad, I was 6!"

"You don't remember the baseball cards I bought you?"

"I don't."

"All right. Thanks for calling."

Though he didn't show it in the call, I knew he was excited for Brett, or at least I hope so.

I often think about that day. I lost my dad on October 13, 2020. There isn't a day that goes by that I don't miss him. He was never a big sports fan and we never had a moment like Brett and I had. On that day I felt like it was three generations of Merkins sharing in a great father-son moment. Cooperstown will always occupy a big place in my heart.

Cal Ripken, Jr.

No one exudes class more than Cal Ripken, Jr. Over the years, I have booked Cal numerous times. The first time was 2010 when Sirius XM reached out to me and asked if Cal and his brother, Billy, could use one of our studios to do their show. I said that was absolutely fine. Cal arrived with Billy and their PR guy, John Maroon. When I was setting them up in their studio, I asked Cal and Billy if they would mind coming on with Waddle and Silvy after he was done. They said that was no problem. The guys were great on the air and over the next few years Cal became a regular once a year with either Carmen and Jurko or Waddle and Silvy. He came to town once a summer because he had a futures game that was played at Wrigley Field. John Maroon would always reach out and ask if we wanted Cal in studio. Of course, we always said yes!

Cal was gracious with his time and was willing to take pictures or sign autographs. There are a couple of things that stand out about my relationship with Cal. One year he was all set to come in studio and at the last second, the station added a remote for Carmen and Jurko at the restaurant Buffalo Wings and Rings. I figured I would have to cancel Cal, so I reached out to John and told him the situation. He got right back to me and asked for the address. I gave it to him, and I warned him that there would most likely be fans there seeking autographs. I told him that we would have security as well. He said, "No problem, Randy. Cal is happy to sign for whoever shows up." There was a big crowd and, as John predicted, Cal signed for everyone, even me!

The other cool story with Cal was something simple. The last time we had him in studio was 2018. I got a call from the front desk saying that I have someone waiting in the lobby. They didn't even know who it was. I got out during a break only to greet Cal. Before I could say anything, he extended his hand and said, "My guy, Randy. How are you doing?" Now, someone probably told him my name beforehand, but the fact that one of the greatest baseball players of all time was being chummy with me was a pretty cool moment. I guess the way you treat people does go a long way.

George Steinbrenner #2

It was the spring of 1995 and baseball was a complete mess. They had already cancelled the World Series in 1994. The owners and the head of the Players Association were meeting at a hotel in Minneapolis. There were some big-name players there, including Tom Glavine and Tony Gwynn. For the owners, there was no bigger name than The Boss, George Steinbrenner. The day of these meetings, Hall of Famer Mickey Mantle had just held a press conference stating that he desperately needed a new liver in order to survive. I decided to call The Boss to see if he would come on to talk about Mickey Mantle.

I called the hotel and asked for George Steinbrenner's room. He answered right away with great energy, "Hello!" I responded, "Mr. Steinbrenner, Sir, how are you?"

"NO, NO, NO!"

"No to what?"

"I know why you are calling! You want me to come to talk about the current negotiations between the owners and the players."

"Actually, Sir, that's not true. I wanted you to come on to talk about Mickey Mantle and the announcement he just made."

"I know how you work. You say one thing and then once I get on the air, you will ask me different questions. I promised the Commissioner that I wouldn't do any interviews."

"Mr. Steinbrenner, I promise you we won't ask anything about the labor negotiations."

"The answer is still no."

With my colleague Jonathan Hood sitting next me, I said, "Mr. Steinbrenner."

"Yes?"

"Mr. Steinbrenner." I paused for a second for dramatic effect and then said, "Do it for the Mick. Do it for the Mick, Mr. Steinbrenner! "

He hesitated then shouted, "Put me on the air!" He called out to someone nearby, "I'm going on the air and I'm doing it for the Mick!"

He went on the air with Mark Gentzkow and Jay Mariotti for fifteen minutes. As promised, every question was about Mickey Mantle.

This is one of my most memorable guest-booking stories for a few reasons. First, I convinced one of the most influential figures in sports to come on to talk the troubles of maybe the greatest Yankee of all time. Second, it proved to me that maybe I had a future at this job!

Torii Hunter

Torii is one of my favorite people in sports. I love booking Torii Hunter since he is a great interview and an even better person. Back when I was working at Sporting News Radio, Torii agreed to do a "weekly" with Bob Berger and Bob Stelton each weekend for free. He was always reliable. One week, he was about to come on and Bob and Bob were talking about our upcoming Fantasy Football draft. Torii said, "Wait a minute. You guys are doing a fantasy football league? I'm in!" They said, "If you join you, have to take it seriously." He said, "Trust me. I will." He was part of the draft and he was active every week. One day I was working at my desk and I saw an email I didn't recognize pop up on my screen. The email said, "Hey Randy, what do you want for Randy Moss?" I said, "Who is this?" He replied, "It's Torii, man." I asked, "What's up, Torii?" He said, "Really - what do you want for Randy Moss?" I am a die-hard Cubs fan and I love the way Torii played center field. So, I said, "Give me Lamont Jordan and Tony Gonzalez and make me a promise that when you are a free agent, you will sign with the Cubs." He said, "Can't do that man. I can't rob home runs in Wrigley!!" I think I still traded him Randy Moss.

Years later, Torii was a free agent. I was now working at ESPN 1000 and I had built a decent relationship with him over the years. I called him up one afternoon and told him we need him to play in Chicago. He laughed and said that he would come on with Waddle and Silvy, which he did while we were live at Ditka's. He was awesome and our audience loved his personality! He was screaming for the White Sox to sign him. Well, Torii didn't sign with the Sox, but he signed with the Angels. I told Silvy the story about Wrigley beforehand and Silvy asked him about the Cubs. Torii responded, "It's true. I can't play for the Cubs!"

Weeks later I reached out to Torii again and he asked, "Why do you want me on? I didn't sign with the Sox." I told him that we just wanted to hear why. He came on with Waddle and Silvy and gave great reasons why he passed on the Sox. He said he called and left a message for Kenny Williams and thanked him for the opportunity. The next day that quote was everywhere in Chicago. Torii Hunter is one of the reasons why this business is so much fun!

NBA BASKETBALL

Kobe Bryant

I had only booked Kobe Bryant once. I was working at One-On-One Sports and one of our reporters got him to talk to us at a McDonald's promotion during the week of the 2001 Super Bowl in New Orleans. When I joined ESPN 1000, it was my goal to get Kobe on the station. I knew it wouldn't be easy. Kobe's demand was through the roof and I knew I needed to have a hook to get him on our shows. Unfortunately, he didn't have a relationship with any of our hosts. My best shot was to try to get him when he was playing against the Bulls. I would email the Lakers PR Director, John Black, twice a year with the same request. He usually responded the next day with the same answer, "Kobe is too busy to do any local radio interviews."

A few years later, I was told that all of Kobe's requests would go through his own PR firm. I started working with them and sent the same request twice a year. His new PR Director, Catherine, gave me the same message that Kobe just didn't have the time. I was persistent and didn't give up. Then, in 2009, I remember exactly where I was when I got the email. I was standing outside the Gap store in Northbrook Court when I checked my phone. I saw that I had a new email with the subject line "Kobe in Chicago." With great anticipation, I opened it. The email stated that Kobe was coming to Chicago in March with the Lakers and he would be doing an appearance with an All-Star after school program. I was asked if we would be interested in doing a radio interview with Kobe. I had to pinch myself before I responded, "Of course!" Over the next couple of days, we exchanged emails to set up a time for the interview the following Friday.

Kobe was going to call in from the team bus once they landed in Chicago. I was a little concerned about the connection and his focus since he would be on the bus with his team. I figured the interview would probably be five minutes and we were certainly going to give a plug about Kobe's appearance for this great cause in Chicago. While I was picking up my kids from school, I was listening on a coupler line on my phone. (Back then, there were no apps to listen to radio stations!) Kobe called in a few minutes late, but you could tell from his very first answer that he was engaged. He was on the air with Carmen Defalco, Harry Teinowitz and Dave Revsine. He spent about twelve minutes with them and was very thoughtful with his answers. While I would expect nothing less from Kobe, I was very relieved that it all went smoothly.

I still couldn't believe that I had finally booked Kobe, one of the greatest athletes in the last half-century. I sent an immediate thank-you email to Catherine. The next day, she asked for a copy of the interview because they wanted to put it up on Kobe's website. I still think about that surprise email and the interview from the bus. I think about how much we, as a society and the sports world, miss Kobe Bryant every day. RIP Kobe.

Dwyane Wade

Dwyane Wade is a Chicago guy. I booked him numerous times when he was on the Miami Heat, usually through a promotion that he was involved with, and he is a great interview. All Bulls fans always dreamed of DWade playing for the Bulls someday.

I was in charge of booking guests for our *Lunch with a Legend* series. This was an hour-long show where the "Legend" would be in person in front of a live audience at Morton's The Steakhouse. I knew DWade still had great ties to Chicago since he did a huge charity weekend through his foundation every summer before the start of the basketball season. I reached out to his contact and asked if we could set up DWade as part of the *Lunch with a Legend* series. Usually we paid our "Legends" and the price varied depending on the person. However, DWade was willing to waive the fee if we would promote his foundation weekend. I agreed and we worked for a couple of weeks to get a date set up. Once we announced Dwyane Wade as a *LWAL* guest, it sold out in less than an hour!

I was pretty psyched. Silvy bought a Bulls jersey with Wade's name on the back that we were going to give him. I was told that a lot of important clients were going to be at this show. As we approached the event, I continued to communicate with Wade's reps about arrival and other information. He was scheduled to be on from 12-1. That morning, I got a text from his PR guy, Adam, who said they were in the Chicago suburb of Robbins for the morning because Dwyane had bought his mom a church and they were there for the presentation. I said, "Congratulations. You still will be here by 11:30 right?" He said, "Absolutely." Well, I got a text at 11 saying they were still in Robbins and should be leaving in fifteen minutes. I asked Adam, "Do you think you will make it by noon?" He said that the latest they would be was 12:15. My stomach dropped! My boss, John Cravens, kept coming up (not knowing that Dwyane was running behind) asking me if we were good. I answered "yes," but not very confidently. Adam texted me at 11:45 that they were just entering the city. I told them to pull up front and I would be waiting. I was freaking out. He then texted me at 11:55 that they were still ten minutes away. I was thinking, Oh no! Maybe they are going to the other Morton's! I was now downstairs waiting for them and texted Jeff Meller, who ran the board, to be ready to start without him. I waited downstairs until 12:05 - no DWade.

I went upstairs getting ready to hear from John about no DWade. I was shocked when I walked and saw Waddle and Silvy interviewing him!!! He had come through the back door. Adam approached me and introduced himself. The hour was amazing! I texted Charles Barkley during a break and asked him to call in. (Back then, DWade and Barkley were doing hysterical commercials.) He called in and gave DWade some crap for being called a "Legend." It was very funny. In the final segment, Silvy presented

DWade with tons of Bulls swag and basically begged him to become a Bull. He got a kick out of it! Little did we know a year later he almost did become a Bull. So, I thought it would be cool to show the behind the scenes of how LWAL worked. Usually the guests showed up on time, but sometimes it came down to the last minute!

Dikembe Mutombo

Dikembe Mutombo has one of the most distinguishable voices in the NBA. He is a gregarious guy both on and off the court. In 1999, The NBA was involved in a lockout and Dikembe Mutombo was one of the voices for the NBA Players Association. News broke that the sides had reached an agreement. The players and management were both staying at a hotel in New York City. I was open to get someone on from both sides, so my first try was Ray Allen. He was awesome since he came on with great info!

I was a little apprehensive to try Dikembe Mutombo. He's sometimes challenging to understand, but he's a huge name. I figured, why not try Dikembe; I bet he's a friendly guy. I called the hotel and asked for his room. He answered right away. I said, "Hey, Dikembe, it's Randy with One-On-One Sports. Congratulations on getting a deal done." He responded, "Thanks, man." I asked if I could I borrow a couple of minutes of his time to talk about the deal. He replied, "Everyone wants a few minutes of Dikembe's time. The NBA wants a few minutes of Dikembe's time. My agent wants a few minutes of Dikembe's time; when is it Dikembe's time???" I said, "Well, can you give us a couple of minutes now and then you can have Dikembe time?" He paused and, thankfully said, "Go ahead, man!" He was very good on the air and has one of the best laughs ever.

FYI, years later, I booked Dikembe during the summer of 2020. I had his email from a few years ago when he was in Chicago and I tried to get him in studio, but that didn't work out. He came on with Carmen and Jurko. He was a little tough to understand, but again, that laugh and sense of humor made it all worthwhile!

Scottie Pippen

Scottie Pippen is the second-greatest Bull of all time. Working in this industry during most of the Bulls Championship run was quite a thrill for a die-hard Bulls fan. When Scottie was a player, I didn't have much interaction with him. However, once he retired, I was able to book him multiple times. Scottie has joined us as a guest more than seven times, including doing a *Lunch with a Legend*. However, there are two stories that stand out.

The first one happened at the Final Four in Indianapolis. Word had leaked that Scottie Pippen was elected to the Hall of Fame, which they always announce at the Final Four. I knew he would be at the press conference they were holding because he was one of the bigger names to go into the Hall. My chances of getting Scottie on the phone weren't great. I figured I would have to find the hotel where Scottie was staying, so after searching through five hotels, I finally found him. (When I say, "searching through hotels to find a guest," I mean literally calling the hotel and asking for Scottie Pippen. I usually look for the bigger hotels like Marriott, Hyatt, Hilton, etc…) After finding Scottie's name, I knew I would probably have a small window to book him.

The press conference was at 11 am. I had it on the TV in the studio and saw that everything finished up around 11:40. I thought it would be a homerun to get Scottie on to lead the noon hour. I called the hotel at 11:59. They rang his room, but I couldn't hear the phone ring. All I heard was music. Then a second later, I heard that distinguishable voice of Scottie's. I congratulated him on making the Hall of Fame and asked if he had a few minutes to join Waddle and Silvy. He said, "Absolutely!" It was probably the friendliest he ever was to me. He came on with the guys and was outstanding while spending ten minutes talking about his career.

The second Scottie Pippen story has to do with him being in studio. Scottie was promoting Giordano's Pizza. Athletes often do this. You give them a few minutes to talk about the product they are promoting, and in return, you get to have them on for an extended time. Scottie was coming into our studios, but the only problem was that Waddle and Silvy were in Bristol. I believe they were filling in for Mike and Mike. Nevertheless, it was an engaging conversation since guests are always better when they are in studio. A couple of weeks before Scottie joined us, he went on with Mike and Mike and said someday LeBron might be the best overall basketball player in NBA History. That made big news considering Scottie was Michael Jordan's teammate. So when he was on, Silvy of course, went there. He asked him about his statement, and it was a good conversation. Then Silvy asked Scottie, "If you had to have one guy by your side to win a title, who you picking- LeBron or MJ?" Scottie got this big smirk on his face and then said, "That has to be the dumbest f****** question anyone has ever asked me." Of course, it led to a big laugh! Scottie's post-NBA career was always a very engaging interview.

One side note - I received a media alert that Scottie was going to be at the opening for Giordano's Pizza in Glenview around five years ago. They asked me if I would like to attend this event on a Sunday night. I said I would love to, but asked if I could bring my kids to meet Scottie. They said, "Sure!" We arrived and the place was jammed. Everyone was outside because the new Giordano's was strictly take-out. We waited in line and my twins, Brett and Dana, got to say and hi and take a picture with Scottie. That was a memorable moment for them!

Michael Jordan

I have never personally booked Michael Jordan, but he is at the top of my list. He's really the "impossible get" for radio producers. He has no interest in doing any radio interviews because he has nothing to gain from it. Even if you have Michael's number, he most likely wouldn't agree to an interview unless you have an angle.

He did come on One-On-One Sports once when he was playing baseball because our stringer, Jerry Kuc, had a great relationship with Michael. He got MJ to do a phone interview during Spring Training. He actually broke news in that interview when he said that if he came back, he would wear number 45 on his jersey.

During the NBA Lockout in 1999, the Players Association set up meetings in Las Vegas. We found out that the players were staying at the Bellagio and I got word that Michael Jordan was listed. I thought, "Why would MJ list his real name?" Anyways, I knew I couldn't just call him and ask him if he had five minutes. That would never work. I went to the President and Majority Owner of One-On-One Sports, Chris Brennan, and explained the situation and I asked if he knew anyone who was friends with MJ. I needed a hook to break the ice, or I had no chance. He told me a good friend of his played golf with Michael at least once every other week and they were tight.

With that information, I called the Bellagio and asked for MJ's room. I had our host, Peter Brown, waiting in the other studio ready to go. Michael answered fairly quickly. I introduced myself and asked how he was doing.

"Fine. What do you need?"

"Actually, we have a mutual friend."

"Oh yeah, who's that?"

I told him the name of the person who he supposedly played golf with all the time. He said that he never heard of him. I asked, "Are you sure? He says you guys play golf all the time." He responded again that he never heard of him! I was not off to a good start. I continued by asking if he might have five minutes to tape an interview to talk about the labor issues in the NBA. He said, "No thanks. I'm just here as moral support for the players."

"I promise we will keep it short."

He said once again, "No, I'm going to take a pass." I knew I only had one more try. I went all in. I said, "Michael if you come on right now, I'll retire. To be quite honest I can't book any bigger guest then you. If you come on, that's it, I'm done."

He chuckled and said, "That's not bad, but the answer is still no." I tried one more time and he finally said, "Ok, this is getting old. Thanks for the offer and take care."

We had one more last-ditch effort. I called Jerry Kuc and asked him to call the hotel room. We conferenced him and the hotel together. MJ's good friend, George Koehler, answered the phone. He also knew Jerry well. He said MJ had just left the room. Well, that was that - no Michael Jordan. I often think of that day and what could have been if he had said "yes." It would have been one of the biggest highlights of my career!

On a side note, I knew from childhood that I was never going to be a great athlete, unfortunately. Once I found my passion in radio, I always thought, "Why not be the Michael Jordan of guest booking?" I don't know what level player I've reached, but I continue to strive to be the best at what I do.

Phil Jackson

Phil Jackson is one of the legendary coaches in NBA history and maybe the best coach of all time. Every time I called him, I was scared to death. I don't know why because he was usually friendly. The history of my relationship with Coach Jackson started when I was working for One-On-One Sports/Sporting News Radio. We owned and operated stations out of New York, LA, and Chicago. Our LA station had the Lakers and also carried *The Phil Jackson Show* hosted by Chris Myers. There was a two-week period where we, in Chicago, had to produce the show. I was going to produce, and Bob Berger was going to host. My instructions were to call Coach Jackson half an hour before the show started. He would then tell me what book he wanted to talk about in the final segment with Bob. When I called Coach Jackson, I could feel my heart racing. The first time I believe Jeanie Buss, his girlfriend and President of the LA Lakers, answered. She was very nice. Coach came on the phone and we went through the show. Not only was it a blast producing the Phil Jackson show, but I also had Phil's home number.

When I started working at ESPN, Coach Jackson was coaching the Lakers. He won his 10th and 11th titles since I started there. I found out that Tom Waddle used to host a show called *The Bulls/Sox Underground* and Phil came on every week. He suggested that instead of doing an interview, they would do a book report every week. Tom told me they had a good relationship. Truth be told, everyone loves Tom Waddle! Well, I decided to call Phil after title 10 at home. He answered with that raspy voice and I was very nervous. The words barely came out of my mouth. I said, "Coach, it's Randy with Tom Waddle.

"Hey Randy. How's Tom doing?"

"Good. Congratulations. Is there any chance you might have time to join his radio show?"

"Sure, just call my secretary tomorrow and she will set it up."

This started a great four-year run where Coach came on several times and even after each championship! You have to understand when Phil Jackson speaks, he's a lot like EF Hutton. Everyone is listening and when he says something newsworthy, it blows up. Case in point, I called Phil late November at home and asked him to come on. He said, "No problem, Randy." I set it up through his office. This was just after LeBron, Wade and Bosh joined together and they were struggling. Silvy is always great at asking the important questions and he asked him about the Heat. Phil said, "Well, if things keep going the way they are going, Coach Spo might have to be replaced by Pat like what happened with Stan Van Gundy!" I knew right away that was gold. It was! It went viral. Coach Spo had to comment on it. The next night I was watching the Heat game on ESPN. They played the cut and Jeff Van Gundy went off.

I lost touch with Coach Jackson after he took the Knicks job. I only spoke to him briefly one other time and he said it was a bad time. However, for a kid who idolized the Jordan Bulls, having a relationship for a while with Phil Jackson is a definite highlight of my career.

Charles Barkley #1

One of my most cherished relationships is the one I have with Charles Barkley. He is the real deal! I first met Charles nearly twenty years ago when I was producing for James Brown. When I moved over to ESPN 1000, he had no reason to continue coming on, or so I thought. It was my understanding that he only came Sporting News Radio because of his relationship with JB. The first week I started with Waddle and Silvy, we were discussing future guests. I told them that I could try Charles Barkley. They both chuckled (no pun intended) and said, "Yeah, good luck." Like Michael Jordan, it lights a fire under me when my hosts question my booking abilities!

David Stern was going to meet the media to discuss the suspension of Tim Donaghy. I thought that this would be the perfect time to get Charles on to address it. He wasn't a big texter back then, so I figured I would have to call him. The presser was at 11am and we were going to carry it live. It was a really big deal. A ref was cheating and that's huge news!

I called Charles on his cell phone. He answered right away. I said, "Charles, it's Randy with ESPN 1000. How are you doing?"

"I'm good."

"I don't know if you remember me, but I used to book you for JB."

"Of course, man! How are you doing?"

I told him that I was great and asked if he would be willing to join my hosts after the commissioner spoke. (Charles had never met neither Waddle nor Silvy.) He said, "Sure. I'll be watching the presser as well. Just call me when he's done." I told the guys, and they were psyched.

As soon as they presser was done, he came on. He was fantastic! I mentioned to both guys that Charles is great talking about anything. We don't have to spend the entire time discussing Donaghy. They veered off to other subjects and it was an amazing interview. At the end, he said to call him anytime. And we did! Over the next four years, Charles was probably on twenty-five times.

In 2011, the Bulls were on a roll. They had beat the Pacers and were now on to the Hawks. We had Charles on before the series started. He said to Waddle and Silvy, "We (TNT) have the Eastern Conference Finals and we are traveling. If the Bulls beat the Hawks, my ass is in studio with you guys for the whole show!" This was it! It was always a goal of mine to get Charles in studio. After each win, I would text Charles with this message: 3 more, 2 more 1 more. Then, when the Bulls clinched, I said "Your ass is coming in studio!" He responded right away, "Yes, Sir." Then, the next text made my stomach sink... "Wait a minute," it read. "Let me clear it with TNT." I thought, "Oh no – we've got no chance." An hour later he texted, "See you next week." I set up all the details and Charles would be in studio from 11-1.

That day, I had *Limo Bill* (he was our Uber before Uber) pick up Charles at the hotel. I met Charles in the lobby of the ABC Building when he arrived. He came out of the SUV larger than life. I shook his hand and thanked him for coming. He probably took ten pictures and signed twenty items in five minutes. As we were walking in, I told him that this means the world to us and is a really big deal for the station. I asked, "Do you mind taking pictures and signing some autographs? He said, "Bro, whatever you want." The following two hours flew by and every break there was a line of 10-15 people wanting to meet him. Not only did he never say "no," but he spoke with each individual like they were friends. I found that quality amazing. I remember Mark Giangreco (from ABC-Ch 7) stuck around to talk with Charles and Waddle and Silvy. When he was done, he also did a TV interview with Lou Canellis (from Fox).

The next day, we sent Charles his favorite cigars and a case of Diet Coke, since he loved it back then. He sent me a text thanking us. Two weeks later, when the Heat were in the finals against the Mavericks, he came on again. During that interview, he ripped the Heat fans and it made national news. Every time Charles comes on a radio show, you never know what he is going to say. He is totally unfiltered and as real as you can get. There will be more stories about Charles later...

Shaquille O'Neal

I have had some dealings with the great Shaquille O'Neal over the years. However, there are a few that stand out. He was always on my list. What list? My list of guests I had to book before I stop producing. As a producer, you always have to look for angles and different ways to book big-name guests. Most likely Shaq would not come on ESPN Chicago unless there was a specific angle or if he was promoting something. I happened to read that Shaq was coming out with a new drink through Arizona Tea. I found the contact number for Arizona Tea and somehow got to the right person. I told him that we were interested in interviewing Shaq about his new drink. The PR person responded and said they had over fifty requests from various outlets, so he would pick the top two. She told me to send an email pleading my case. I did just that and two weeks later I got the response. Shaq had picked ESPN Chicago and ESPN LA! I reached out to the Executive Producer at ESPN LA, David Singer, and asked him how that happened. He was in shock as well.

The PR person told me to give her all the particulars, including the name of the hosts, the hotline number, and my cell as a backup. He was scheduled to call in at 5:30pm on a Wednesday with Waddle and Silvy. I was driving home, and I had just pulled into a convenient store parking lot when I got a call from a private number on my cell. I answered the phone and I hear, "Randy Merkin, it's Shaq." Then he made some cheering sound. I said, "Shaq, you called the wrong number. You called my cell and you need to call the hotline."

He was pretty funny and said, "Maybe I want to talk with you, Randy Merkin," and then he made that cheering noise again. I said "Shaq, then our audience won't be able to hear you. Give me your cell and we will call you." He laughed and said, "No, give me *your* hotline and I will call you."

He called and was very engaging. He was great about the Bulls, NBA and had fun with Waddle and Silvy. Around 6 minutes into the interview he asked, "How come I haven't heard from the lovely Silvia yet??" Silvy then responded, "No, Shaq. Silvia is actually me, Silvy." He laughed and said, "Oh, that's funny." The interview went for another couple of minutes and then, at the end, Silvy said, "Ok, Shaquira. Thanks for coming on!" Shaq got a big kick out of that.

My other encounter with Shaq is a totally different story. As a station, we were headed to Cleveland to cover the Cubs in the World Series. We took a party bus that included most of the on-air staff and our GM, Jim Pastor, and Program Director, Adam Delevitt. We left at around 7pm central time. It was quite the trip. I will leave it at this - boys will boys! So we finally arrived at the hotel in Cleveland around 3am eastern time and we were all exhausted. We get in two lines to check in and I was the last one in line. I turned to my right and see a few people walking into the hotel. I could barely open my eyes, but I recognized Shaq walking in! I hit Jeff Meller on his shoulder and said, "It's Shaq, it's Shaq! Come on!" I go running over and say, "Shaq, Shaq I need a picture with you." He said, "What's up, bro?" I had to use Jeff's phone because my phone was dead, but he was happy to take the picture. We exchanged pleasantries and he went up to his room.

I was thinking that this was going to be a great trip. The reason Shaq was there was because TNT was staying at our hotel for The Cavs banner unveiling, which happened the same night as game 1 of the World Series. We ate breakfast right next to Chris Webber and Marv Albert. Waddle and Silvy hung out with Charles Barkley. It was quite the week!

Jerry Krause

I had a difficult time deciding whether to write this story because I hate to speak ill of the dead. However, I must be honest in saying I never had one good dealing with Jerry Krause. He always treated me with very little respect. The first incident happened back in 1995 when Michael Jordan had returned and was in the middle of a battle against the Magic in the playoffs. Our main host at the time was Ted Green and whatever Ted said, you did. He told me, "Randy, call Jerry Krause and tell him Teddy Ballgame wants to do an interview with him." You can't make this up. I asked, "He knows who you are?" He said, "Oh, ya. He loves me."

I found where the Bulls were staying, and I called the hotel and asked for Jerry Krause's room. He answered with that gruff voice and I said, "Mr. Krause, it's Randy Merkin with Ted Green. How are you?"

"Who?!"

"Ted Green. He says he knows you."

"I have never heard of him. What do you want?"

"Ted wanted to know if you might have 5-10 minutes to tape an interview with him right now?"

"So, let me get this straight. You want me to stop my high-level meeting I'm having right now with Jerry Reinsdorf and Phil Jackson and do an interview with some guy named Ted Green? That might be one of the most unprofessional things I have ever heard."

"I apologize, Mr. Krause, please go back to your meeting."

"What's your name?" he demanded.

I told him my full name. He said, "Do you know how rude you are for interrupting our meeting?!" This went on for several more minutes. I finally said, "I'm going to hang up now." He really made me feel like I did something wrong. I don't mind getting yelled at, but I felt like he made it personal. Weeks later he approached our reporter at the UC and said he felt terrible for the way he treated me and apologized.

The second Jerry Krause incident came in the later summer of 2009. Jerry made a big stink about not going to Michael Jordan's Hall of Fame speech because his good friend and former Bulls assistant, Coach Tex Winter, had not been elected to the Hall. Truth be told, Michael Jordan didn't invite Jerry Krause to his Hall of Fame ceremony. Jerry's quotes made big news in the local newspapers, so I called Jerry at home to see if he would come on. I told him that I was with Waddle and Silvy from ESPN 1000. He seemed very upset and said, "Do you think it is all right to call someone at home?" I apologized and explained we were just looking for clarification about his comments. That didn't sit well with him. He asked for my name and I told him it. Then he asked if I like my job and I said that I did. He asked, "Do you know who Bruce Levine is?"

"Sure, Bruce is a colleague."

"Well, I'm about to call him and tell him how rude you are."

"Well, that's your choice."

He hung up. Minutes later, Bruce called and asked why I called Jerry at home. I told him that I was just doing my job, which Bruce understood. As a producer, sometimes you have to wear it and you will get chewed out or called names. My philosophy is that as long as you show respect to the person you are calling, there is no reason to be a jerk!

A year or so later, I called Jerry again for a Hall of Fame related matter. I was nervous to call him because of how he treated me in the past and it turned out I was right to be nervous. Again, he lectured me and said I was rude for calling him at home and asked if I like my job. He was going to call Bruce to complain about me again. I had enough of his poor treatment towards me. I told him, "Mr. Krause, I am just doing my job. Don't threaten me. I am a good and decent person. I have treated you with respect and I'm just asking that you do the same." He responded that he was going to call Bruce. I know he wasn't always treated fairly during his time in Chicago, but he never did himself any favors by the way he treated others.

Charles Barkley #2

There are so many great stories about Charles Barkley and this one involves when he was a guest on our *Lunch with a Legend series*. Charles called in when Dwyane Wade was our LWAL and provided seven minutes of outstanding radio. The next time we had Charles on with Waddle and Silvy, he asked, "Hey, how come you guys have never asked me to participate in a LWAL?" Of course, the guys told him that he has an open invitation. So, the guys went back and forth with Charles for a few years, but were never able to set anything up. Finally, Waddle and Silvy made a bet with Charles. If they won, he had to do LWAL. They won! I tried numerous times to set up a time with Charles to do the show. Finally, I sent him a text saying, "Hey no big deal, but with the Bears season starting, we want to wrap up LWAL for the season. Just let me know if this year works for you or not."

I remember where I was when I got the text. It was during the Jay Cutler show that Charles texted, "Hey bro, how about Monday, October 11th? That's right before my season begins." I called Adam Delevitt, our Program Director, over and showed him the text. He said to let him confirm it, but it should be a go. It was! I texted Charles back, "Great, let's do it. We will take care of air fare and, before I could say anything else, he said to just pick him up at his hotel and he's got the rest. I said, "Wow, thanks. We will provide a car service for you." He said that sounded good.

We announced the LWAL on air and gave out the number for Morton's The Steakhouse. It usually takes up to a day or two to come close to a sell-out. This one took around fifteen minutes. Then they started selling standing-room only. I was psyched! As we got closer, I started texting Charles for his flight info and other particulars. There was one slight issue. He stopped responding! I would send him texts and receive no response. We were basically a week out and I was freaking out! I was ready to go into my GM's office, Jim Pastor, and tell him that we had to cancel the show.

I was driving home that night when I received a text from Charles. He said, "Sorry bro. I was with my mom for a week. I always turn off my phone when I'm with her. I will send you my flight info and what is the dress code?" I was so relieved. He sent me the flight info and we were all set. His flight was scheduled to arrive Saturday morning. I got a call from our driver, who we call Limo Bill. He said, "Hey Randy, Charles wasn't on the flight you gave me." I was thinking, Oh no! I texted Charles and asked if he missed his flight. He responded, "Sorry, I forgot to text you. I took an early flight and I'm already at the hotel!" Phew! I was relieved that we were all set.

The day of the show arrived. I had Limo Bill all set to pick up Charles around 10am. He was scheduled to be on from 11-1. Limo Bill texted me at 9:30 and said, "Hey, I just picked up Charles we are on our way. He wanted to get there early." I wasn't surprised since that is who Charles is. He showed up around 10:15. I walked him into a side room where we had about fifteen basketballs for him to sign. Of course, he signed every one. He looked at a picture from the last time he was in studio and said, "Man, I was a fat-ass back then!"

I asked if he was ready to go on with the guys and he said, "Let's do it." He went on at 10:23. The place was already packed and you could feel the buzz in the room. I remember at the first break I turned around and there was a line of about fifty people waiting to meet Charles for an autograph. I announced, "Sorry guys. Nothing today." However, he told me to let them all through and he signed for everyone! I mean everyone. Not only did he sign, but he talked to every person, listened to their stories, and was engaged. That's who Charles Barkley is. It was 2 ½ hour of pure gold.

After we were done, I felt bad, but I asked Charles if he minded doing a 30-minute meet & greet with clients before leaving for the airport. He said, "Lead the way." He went back into the side room and signed and talked to everyone who approached him. He finally finished up with that and asked me, "Hey bro. Am I done?"

"You are, and I can't thank you enough."

He took his bag and went to the bathroom. Five minutes later, he returned wearing a sweet sweat suit. He looked at Adam Delevitt, Elena Angelos and me and said, "This is how I travel." And with that, Limo Bill took him to the airport. This is one of my most memorable days in my career. I love Charles Barkley.

Side note: I had my in-laws bring Brett and Dana to meet Charles. They were in kindergarten at the time. Dana and my father-in-law took a picture with him, but Brett was too scared!

COLLEGE BASKETBALL

Rick Pitino

It was April of 1997 and Coach Pitino had just won the National Championship with Kentucky. Coach Pitino was always tough to get on the radio because he was in such high demand. I had reached out to Kentucky Sports Information, but they told me Coach wasn't available because he was going on vacation and then would be recruiting. I understood that and tried to book someone else from the Championship team instead.

I was producing Bob and Bruce's show on a Sunday when I received a call from my boss, Mark Gentzkow. He was with his family at a resort in Sea Island, Georgia. He told me that Coach Pitino had just walked by and was headed to the elevator. It seemed so random that they were at the same resort. I couldn't believe it. "Call him in his hotel room and get him on with Bob and Bruce!" he shouted. I was always a little leery of calling someone while they were on vacation, but this was probably my only chance to reach Coach Pitino.

I looked up the resort's phone number and called and asked for Coach Pitino's room. I wasn't sure exactly how this was going to go. Coach answered pretty quickly. I said, "Hey, Coach, it's Randy Merkin with One-On-One Sports. Congratulations!" You can usually tell right away whether you have a chance by the initial response. I could tell immediately that things didn't look good. Coach asked me in a tone that seemed very agitated, "How did you know I was here?" I told him that my boss was staying in the same resort and had just walked by him. I continued, "Coach, is there any chance you might be willing to join my hosts for a few minutes to talk about winning the National Championship?"

"Here's what I want you do. I want you to hang up the phone right now and never f***** call me on vacation again! Are we clear?!"

"We are clear, Coach." He hung up. Years later, Coach Pitino would join our station, but it was when he was a broadcaster for CBS and Tim Brando set it up!

Jim Boeheim

I have to admit that I have always been afraid of Jim Boeheim. I never had any luck booking him as a guest. I worked during a couple of Sunday nights of *Selection Sunday*, which is usually a very happy time for most college coaches. We would send requests to PR directors on Sunday mornings, but for the bigger-name coaches like Jim Boeheim, we would usually try them directly since that was our best chance to get them on the air. One year, Coach Boeheim had a great team and they were a 1 or 2 seed. Since we were having a great show with coaches, I figured that Coach Boeheim would put us over the top. I called his office and I never even got to Coach Boeheim. I was told he wasn't doing interviews. I thought about trying his cell phone but figured there was no chance.

This brings us to March 12, 2009. Syracuse was to face off against UConn. It was quite the matchup and the game went to 6 overtimes! The game lasted until March 13th. I knew the next day would be all about getting Coach Boeheim on our show. I have to admit, I had some apprehension since I never had any luck with Coach Boeheim. I also heard that sometimes he could be downright mean. It took me a while, because there are so many hotels in New York City, but I finally found where Syracuse was staying. I figured Coach probably got back to his hotel room around 3 am. Waddle and Silvy were on from 9am-12pm. I was a little nervous to call him that early, but I know college coaches during this time. They don't sleep! I tried him starting at 9:30am. There was no answer the first few times that I called. I had his cell number, so I figured why not try his cell as well? Still no answer! I was very curious... If I actually spoke with him, would he be friendly or upset that I called him? All of sudden, right around 11:10am, I saw the hotline ringing and it was Coach Boeheim's cell. I thought to myself that this could get ugly. He could be calling to chew me out for waking him up.

I answered the phone "ESPN 1000, this is Randy." He said, "Hey, Randy. I saw I just missed a call from this number. What did you need?" I said, "Congratulations! What a win! Is there any chance you have a few minutes to join us to talk about that game?" He asked if I meant right then and I told him that yes, right then would be great. He said, "I would be happy to come on." Waddle, Silvy and Mark Giangreco were hosting and Coach Boeheim was engaged. They asked him what he did when he got back to the hotel. He said, "I watched Slumdog Millionaire."

Mission accomplished! I went into the show with the sole purpose of getting Jim Boeheim on and, I did it. Two days later, Stephen Bardo was filing in on Carmen, Jurko and Harry and he said, "Hey man, who the hell got Jim Boeheim on?? That is one hell of a get!" That felt good.

By the way, since 2009, Coach Boeheim has been on multiple times. He is actually a very friendly guy and always a thoughtful interview.

John Calipari

Coach Cal is a producer's dream. He is usually available for interviews and he is a great quote! I have had many experiences with Coach Cal but will detail two of them. The first goes back to when the Bulls got the number one pick. The night of the draft lottery, I texted Coach Cal and said that the Bulls were getting Derrick Rose and asked if he could join us the next day. He responded right away "YES!" We worked out a time and the next day he came on to start the show. His enthusiasm for Derrick was terrific. Throughout Derrick's career, anytime the fans or media would go after him, I would send Coach a text. I would simply say, "They are going after Derrick; can you come on?" He would respond, "When?" If you are one of Cal's guys, he would defend you to the end.

The other Cal memory has nothing to do with booking him as a guest, but more about what kind of person he is. My son's friend lost his father to cancer. They were both huge Kentucky fans. I asked Coach Cal if he would consider signing a basketball to my son's friend. He responded right away saying, "This is done." He also asked if I could provide some information about the young man because he wanted to write a personal note. When you watch Coach Cal on TV, you see a vociferous guy who is full of life. What you don't see is what a great heart he has as well.

Jim Calhoun

Jim Calhoun is one of the greatest college basketball coaches of all time. However, he was never very friendly to the media. He had a run of winning three titles in nine years. He won his last championship with Kemba Walker, which pretty much surprised everyone. Earlier that year, he had a cantankerous relationship with the media. As a matter of fact, he told a few media members to shut up.

The Tuesday morning after UConn won the national title, I told Waddle and Silvy that I found the hotel where Coach Calhoun was staying and I was going to try him throughout the show. They were convinced that there was no way he would say yes. I called the hotel and asked for Coach Calhoun's room. The hotel operator told me that he had a "do not disturb" on his phone for at least another hour. I called back an hour later and they said, "Sorry, he still has a DND on his phone." I said, "Do me a favor and tell him it's ESPN Chicago calling for him." The hotel operator said he would. A few seconds later, I heard that familiar gruff voice saying, "Hello."

"Coach, it's Randy with ESPN 1000. Congratulations."

He kind of chuckled and asked, "How did you find me, Randy?"

"It took a while, but I finally figured out where you were staying. Is there any chance I can convince you to join my guys for a few minutes?"

"I really don't feel like doing any media."

"Come on Coach, just five minutes."

He paused and said, "Ok, go ahead."

"Coach, one more thing. You aren't going to tell Waddle and

Silvy to shut up, are you?"

He laughed and said, "I can't promise anything!"

He was actually very engaging in the interview. The guys brought up that incident with the media and he laughed it off. As a guest booker, there is always no bigger thrill then getting one of the stars of the game on the day after the event. Working at a local station, that is pretty much our only chance. If I went through UConn PR, I might have set up an interview with Coach Calhoun something like two months in the future. If you don't get him the day after, it loses some of the buzz. That is why radio is both great and tough at the same time. The immediacy is such a rush.

Bo Ryan

One of the cool things about my job is the relationships that I build. I am proud to call Bo Ryan a friend. I covered him during my first radio job in Platteville, Wisconsin and my first real encounter with Coach Ryan came in his office. I was going to host his Coaches show. As I went in, I was thinking, "Great, I'm going to interview a division 3 coach each week." I have to admit I didn't do my homework on Bo Ryan, as I knew very little about him. Two minutes into the interview, I said, "Don't you aspire for more than being the head coach of a division 3 team?" He said, "Turn off your tape recorder." Yes, this was 1993 and I was using a tape recorder. He said, "Do you know anything about me?"

"Not really."

"Did you know that I was the lead assistant at Wisconsin for over 5 years? Do you know my work with USA basketball?"

I felt like an idiot. I told him that I knew none of that. He chuckled and said, "Well, maybe next time you will be more prepared."

That was an early lesson in my broadcasting career that I have never forgotten. Over the nine months that I spent in Platteville, I always made a point to stop by his office at least once a week to say hi. I really valued his opinion and I thought a lot of Coach Ryan. After I left Platteville, I made sure to send him letters, and later on, texts to check in. I told all my Wisconsin friends that Bo would be the perfect coach for the Badgers and that he can get them their elusive title.

Well, he eventually did become the head coach of the Badgers. I called him in the hotel in Minneapolis at the Final Four. Sporting News Radio was there doing shows all week. I said, "Coach, it's Randy Merkin. Congratulations!"

"Hey Randy! How are you doing?"

"You have to come join us over at our set at the convention center."

He said that he would and, an hour later, he was there. He gave me a big hug and said that it was great to see me. I congratulated him on becoming the Badgers' head coach. He asked how long we needed him for the interview and said that he was available as long as we wanted. We kept him an hour with Bob and Bruce. We also had other coaches on with him from the Big Ten. I'm not sure everyone listening loved it, but for that hour, I didn't care. As he left, he gave me his cell and said to call him any time.

Well, over the years I called a lot. After a big win, he was on the next day. During the Badgers 2-year-run of Final Four appearances, I texted him after each win. He always responded. In 2007, I was between jobs and I went to the Big Ten Tourney final at the UC when the Badgers were playing Ohio State. The Ohio State team was loaded with Greg Oden and Mike Conley, Jr. to name a few. Sadly, they took care of the Badgers. I was hesitant to go into the locker room to say hi after the game, but I wanted to show Coach Ryan the pictures of my newborn twins, Brett and Dana. I walked in and was waiting for him to finish a conversation. He saw me and came over and gave me a hug. We talked for a minute and I showed him the pictures of Brett and Dana. It meant a lot that he took the time to chat. Sadly, Coach Ryan's departure wasn't great, and I lost touch with him over the last five years. However, I will always treasure our friendship and what he did for me professionally and personally.

Rick Majerus and Al Maguire

Rick Majerus was the head coach of the Utah Utes, and I knew that he was always a fantastic interview. He lived an interesting life. Coach Majerus resided in a hotel in Salt Lake City. If you ever wanted to book him as guest, you called his hotel room. Most of the time you would leave a message and he would call back and say he was more than willing to do the interview on one condition - he wanted at least fifteen minutes to talk basketball and a mere five-minute-interview was not enough. We were always willing participants and I respected Coach Majerus since he had such a passion for both his job and for college hoops.

The Utah Utes were on quite a roll in 1998 and they were loaded with Keith Van Horn and Andrew Miller leading the team. All they had to do was beat the top-seeded Arizona team and they were in the Final Four! This would be the first time for Coach Majerus. In the second half of the game, it looked good for them to make the Final Four. I called our stringer and said, "I want Coach Majerus after the game." Utah Sports Information was a great help to the stringer. He called back ten minutes later and told me it was set, but it would probably be an hour after the game. Our host at that time was the great Larry Cotlar, AKA the "Cot Man." I informed him that he would have Coach Majerus and he was psyched.

I figured most national networks were going to have Coach and wondered how we could make the interview different. How could we make it stand out? Then it hit me. In our May interview with Coach Majerus, I remembered that he spoke about how much he loved his dad who was no longer with him. However, he said that he always thought of Coach Al Maguire as his second dad. Coach had been on his staff at Marquette and knew him well. What if I put

Coach Maguire on with Coach Majerus? I called Coach Maguire and ran the idea past him. He said, "Sure! I would love to say hi to Ricky."

I let the "Cot Man" know what was going on. I told him I would call Coach Maguire when there were three minutes left in the interview. He loved the plan. So, Coach Majerus called in and was on with Larry. The interview was going well. I called Coach Maguire and told him Coach Majerus was on the air with Larry Cotlar. He said, "I'm ready to congratulate Ricky." I put him on hold and told Larry. Larry told Coach Majerus, "Before you go, we have a very special guest who wants to say hi." The next voice was Al Maguire saying, "Ricky." Coach Majerus was shocked and so happy. He said, "Coach Maguire, is that you?"

"Ricky, congratulations!"

"Thanks, Coach." They talked for a minute about his game plan. I could tell Coach Maguire was getting ready to say goodbye, but before he did, he told his friend, "Ricky, your dad would be so proud of you!" Coach Majerus broke down and started crying. I mean, uncontrollable weeping. Coach Maguire, not missing a beat, said, "All right, Ricky, love you" and hung up, leaving Larry to deal with a crying Coach Majerus.

Coach composed himself and thanked Larry for that special moment. I remember that Larry said goodbye on the air and that this was probably the coolest moment he had been involved with. The toughest part of this story is that all three people are no longer with us. They were great people, were amazing to work with and it was an honor to know them.

Randy with Rapper, Snoop Dog, in the ESPN 1000 studio in 2018.

Randy with Bears great and University of Michigan Coach, Jim Harbaugh, at Chicago Cut Steakhouse in 2016.

Randy with Cubs Hall of Famer, Ryne Sandberg, at Busch Stadium in St. Louis in 2016.

Randy with NFL Hall-of-Fame Coach, Tony Dungy, in the ESPN 1000 Studio in 2019.

PHOTOS

Randy with MLB great, Pete Rose, at Morton's The Steakhouse in 2015.

Randy with NBA Hall of Famer, Charles Barkley, at Chicago Cut Steakhouse in 2020.

Randy with Heavyweight Champ, Evander Holyfield, in the ABC Building in 2017.

Randy with MLB Hall of Famer, Cal Ripkin Jr., in the ESPN 1000 Studio in 2019.

Randy with NBA Hall of Famer, Shaquille O'Neal, in the lobby of a Cleveland hotel in 2016.

Randy with Rocco Mediate at a Champions golf event in Highland Park in 2019.

Randy with Larry King in the ESPN 1000 Studio in 2015.

Randy with Blackhawks Hall of Famer, Chris Chelios, at Morton's The Steakhouse in 2014.

PHOTOS

Randy with NBA Hall of Famer, Alonso Mourning, in the ESPN 1000 Studio in 2010.

Randy with Cubs Pitcher, Jake Arrieta, at Chicago Cut in 2015.

Randy with NFL star, Drew Brees, in the ESPN 1000 Studio in 2016.

Randy with Cub great, Kyle Schwarber, in the ESPN 1000 Studio in 2016.

BEHIND THE GLASS: STORIES FROM A SPORTS RADIO PRODUCER

Randy with NBA Hall of Famer, Kareem Abdul-Jabbar, in the ESPN 1000 Studio in 2016.

Randy with Cubs Owner, Tom Ricketts, in the ESPN 1000 Studio in 2016.

Randy with Cubs Pitcher, Kyle Hendricks, in the ESPN 1000 Studio in 2017.

Randy with Scottie Pippen in the ESPN 1000 Studio in 2012.

PHOTOS

Randy with Carlos Boozer in the ESPN 1000 Studio in 2019.

Randy with Big Cat at the ESPN Fantasy Football Convention in 2018.

Randy's twins with Bulls Hall of Famer, Scottie Pippen, at a Giordano's opening in 2016.

Randy's daughter, Dana, and Father-in-law, Bob Tarschis, with Charles Barkley at Morton's The Steakhouse in 2012.

Randy with Jurko, Carmen and Henry Winkler, The Fonz, in the ESPN 1000 Studio in 2019.

PHOTOS

Randy with Heavyweight Champ, Mike Tyson, in the ESPN 1000 Studio in 2011.

Randy with Heavyweight Champ, Mike Tyson, in the ESPN 1000 Studio in 2013.

BEHIND THE GLASS: STORIES FROM A SPORTS RADIO PRODUCER

Randy, his twins and Bulls player, Jimmy Butler, in the ESPN 1000 Studio in 2013.

Randy with Blackhawks Coach Quenneville and The Stanley Cup in the ESPN 1000 Studio 2013.

PHOTOS

Brett & Dana Merkin with Bears Hall of Famer, Brian Urlacher, at Ditka's in 2016.

Randy with his 2 "holes in one" shadow box.

67

Brett's DYBA 12U Red baseball team at Cooperstown in 2019.

Randy with his son, Brett, at Cooperstown in 2019.

NFL FOOTBALL

Peyton Manning

Any good guest booker would want to have Peyton Manning on their show. I am fortunate to have booked Peyton Manning a few times - once when he was at the University of Tennessee and another when I reached him at the Pro Bowl Hotel in Hawaii. He was a guest on the "Troy Aikman Show," which I produced on Sporting News Radio. As the years went by, however, I realized that it was getting more difficult to book Peyton Manning. Unless you had a hook or unless Peyton knew your hosts well, you probably weren't going to book him.

Brian Urlacher announced his retirement from football in 2014. I read that Peyton and Brian had become good friends and I knew that Peyton would often write a note of congratulations to a player that had recently retired. Over the years, I had obtained Peyton's email address, but when I emailed, he never responded. I figured this would be a prime opportunity to book Peyton and I had a hook - Brian Urlacher. I sent Peyton an email one evening asking if he could come on for a few minutes to talk about Brian Urlacher retiring. The following morning around 7am, I received an email from the Denver Broncos PR Staff. It read that Peyton would be happy to come on to strictly talk about Brian retiring. He was going to call at 12:10pm and needed to be done by 12:16. At the end of the email, it advised, "In the future, please send all requests for Peyton to the Denver Broncos." I replied, "No problem," gave them the hotline number where Peyton should call and thanked them.

Not surprisingly, Peyton called at 12:09:30. He was extremely polite and thanked me for the opportunity to come on and talk about his good friend, Brian Urlacher. Peyton was going on the air with Waddle and Silvy. He had never been on with them since I was their producer, and he didn't know either one. In fact, we had Archie Manning on the show years before and it was a long-standing joke on our show because Archie said to Tom, "Tom, you know Peyton!" but Tom shook his head no. (He probably assumed this because Tom was a professional football player.) Now Peyton was actually on with Waddle and Silvy. The interview went very well, and he stayed on longer than expected. He spoke about his many battles against Brian and how much he enjoyed them. When the guys wrapped up, I picked up the phone to thank Peyton and, again, he thanked *me* for having *him*.

The final twist to this story was that I had already booked *The Great One*, Wayne Gretzky, to come on the show at 12:15pm. So, we went from one of the top five QBs of all time to the best hockey player of all time. Talk about a cool transition!

Coach Parcells and Drew Bledsoe

Super Bowl week is always an extremely exciting time for the football world and the sports media world. The Packers had made it to their first Super Bowl with Brett Favre as Quarterback and they were going to face Bill Parcells, Drew Bledsoe, and the Patriots. I was producing on the Sunday when both teams arrived in New Orleans. I looked up on the TV screen and saw that the Patriots' plane had just landed, so I told Bob Berger and Bruce Murray be ready in thirty minutes. I was going to call some of the Patriots in their hotel rooms. First, I needed to find their hotel. It took me four tries, but I finally found where the team was staying.

It was around 5:30pm when I started calling the Patriots in their hotel rooms. Sports Sunday ended at 6pm, so I basically had thirty minutes. I figured I might as well start at the top and the first person I tried was Bill Parcells. He answered on the fourth ring. I said, "Coach, it's Randy Merkin with One-On-One Sports. Congratulations! How are you doing?" There was silence for a few seconds and then he shouted, "Oh boy! It's starting already," and hung up on me. After that first miss, I decided I could either give up or try the next best player. (Oddly enough, around eight years later, Bruce Murray became the co-host of the Bill Parcells show on Sporting News Radio.)

I shook off the Coach Parcells hang up and decided to call Drew Bledsoe. He answered on the first ring. I gave him the same warm greeting and asked if he might have five to ten minutes to join the show.

"Absolutely! Do you need me to go downstairs?" I told him that we could do the interview right over the phone.

"Great, go ahead and put me on." He ended up spending ten minutes with Bob and Bruce.

Think about this - one week before Drew's biggest game, he was on the air with One-On-One Sports. I'm fairly certain that we were the first radio interview he did because when I called, he told me that he had just entered his hotel room. As a producer, there's no bigger rush than getting a big-name guest for the Super Bowl!

Bill Walsh

In the late 90's, calling hotels was the main way to book guests. The NFL Combine was usually a goldmine since NFL GMs and Coaches all held up in their hotel rooms. Back in 1999, there were rumblings of a trade that was close to happening between the 49ers and Redskins. Hall-of-Fame Coach Bill Walsh had transitioned from being the head of the 49ers to then being their President and General Manager. From my past dealings with Coach Walsh, he was always a very friendly man. I figured why not give him a try? The worst thing he could say was "no," right?

I called the hotel in Indy and asked for his room. Coach answered right away, and I said, "Hey Coach, it's Randy with One-On-One Sports. How are you doing?"

"Great, Randy. How can I help you?"

"Is there any chance you can join us for five minutes?"

"Sure, no problem."

I told him that we wanted to ask him about the proposed trade with the Redskins. What he said next still blows me away.

"Randy," Coach Walsh said, "Oh, it's no longer proposed. We just completed the trade, and I would be more than happy to talk about it." From my experience, coaches and GMs are never this transparent. I was in shock.

I put Coach Walsh on with Bob and Bruce. I typed on the screen that the trade was done, so they asked him about it, and he delved right into this newsworthy topic. He was of the opinion that the Redskins probably got the better end of the deal, but that it was still best for them to make the trade. Bob and Bruce began asking Coach Walsh about their starting QB. "Well, we got this young kid named Jeff Garcia. I don't think he can play, but we really have no other options." The honesty that Coach Walsh demonstrated with us was remarkable.

The fallout from the interview was pretty big. You have to remember that back in 1999, we didn't have Twitter or Facebook. If you were able to get on ESPN, that was huge publicity for your station. So, we edited the interview and sent it to SportsCenter, which used it. We also transcribed all the pertinent quotes and sent them to the beat writers for both the Redskins and 49ers. They used it as well. I never thought Coach Walsh would even do the interview, much less give us such a big scoop!

Harry Carson

Harry Carson was a great linebacker for the Giants, and he was on an elite defense with Lawrence Taylor. Most NFL experts thought he was worthy of making the Hall of Fame. However, he had been up for the Hall for years and had not made it yet. It became a yearly thing to debate whether or not this was the year that Harry Carson would finally make the Hall of Fame.

For about an 8-year period, I was always producing on Saturday when the Hall made their announcements. It was one of the cooler parts of my job to call players to tell them they made the it. A few times I even beat Joe Horrigan, President of the Football Hall of Fame, to be the first to tell the player he made it. Probably one my favorite memories was telling Bear great Mike Singletary that he had made the Hall.

On this Saturday in 2002, we were doing our show from Leigh Steinberg's Super Bowl party at the San Diego Zoo. It was Bob Stelton, Bob Berger, and Jim Mora. That year, we had all come to the conclusion that the locks for the Hall were Marcus Allen and Hank Stram. We had a producer back in the studio in Northbrook ready to relay to me who made it. We had a reporter just outside the voting for the Hall of Fame that would give us the new inductees first. I heard the producer talking to our insider about some potential people who had made it. He said, "Ok, Randy, here's the list who made it." Harry Carson was on the list! However, both Marcus Allen and Hank Stram were not. I said to him, "Are you sure this is the list?" He said it is confirmed 100 percent. I gave the list to the guys. They were very critical of the committee. How could they not put in Marcus Allen and Hank Stram? Hank was very sick, and this was probably his last chance to make while he was living.

So, as soon I heard that Harry Carson made the Hall of Fame, I called his cell phone. I said, "Harry, congratulations, you made the Hall!"

"I did?"

I said, "I just got the list!" He yelled to what seemed to be a large crowd at his house, "I made it!" They went crazy. I asked, "Can I call you from a different number and put you on the air?" He said, "Randy, let me wait until I hear from Joe Horrigan. I promise you that once I hear from Joe, you are the first interview I'm doing." I said, "Great!" and hung up.

Literally five minutes later, I heard the producer down the line say, "Oh wait - that's the list of the players that have been eliminated?" I yelled, "Tell me you are joking!"

"No, I guess I gave you the wrong list."

"I can't believe it! What are you doing?!" I asked.

"Ok, here's who made the Hall..." Bob and Bob could tell something was up. I printed out the new list and gave it to them. They couldn't believe it either. They said, "We owe everyone an apology. We gave you the wrong list for the Hall."

That's why it doesn't matter if you are first or not, but just be right! Bob, Bob, and Coach Mora brought up that once again Harry Carson didn't make the Hall. I thought, "Oh my gosh! I had just called him and told him he made it!"

I had to call Harry Carson and apologize. It was probably one the most nerve-wracking calls I have ever had to make. He answered right away with a somber tone. I said, "Harry, it's Randy calling back from Sporting News Radio. I am so sorry. I jumped the gun. You didn't make the Hall of Fame. It is totally my fault." He graciously said, "Randy please don't worry about it. It's not the first time this has happened." I again apologized and said I felt terrible.

"Please don't worry about it." That was the end of conversation. I thought, thank goodness Harry had the smarts to not come on the radio until he received official confirmation that he had made the Hall.

Terry Bradshaw

One of the all-time great quarterbacks and one of the best NFL analysts, Terry Bradshaw, made his mark in the NFL. Terry was always in high demand for interviews, but rarely did many unless he was promoting something.

I was lucky enough to book Terry a few times when I worked at Sporting News Radio. He worked with JB when JB was at Fox, so I had Terry's numbers from him. When I left Sporting News Radio, I thought I wouldn't have much of a chance to book Terry anymore, but that didn't stop me from trying!

I had the number for his ranch in Louisiana and I wanted to put Terry on with Waddle and Silvy. I must have tried his number twenty times over the span of a few weeks, but he never answered. Finally, one afternoon, he answered. He wasn't too friendly but told me he was busy and to call him the following morning at 7am. He said after that he will be working on the farm the rest of the day. I called the following morning around 7am and Terry answered. He must have forgotten that we had a conversation the day before because he let me have it! He wanted to know why I would call him so early and said that he's not coming on under any circumstances. I didn't put up much resistance. I thanked him for his time and hung up. Five minutes later he called back and apologized. He said that I caught him at a bad time, and he would be happy to join us. We worked out a time for him to join Waddle and Silvy.

    I set up Terry on a Thursday. Waddle and Silvy always did their show on Thursdays from Ditka's restaurants during the football season. I remember Terry was right on time and had a ton of energy. However, during the interview all three of us noticed a few times that Terry was out of breath. We were actually getting concerned. Towards the end of the interview Silvy asked, "Terry, are you ok? You seem to be out of breath." Terry laughed and told us during the entire interview he was on the treadmill and he started ramping up his speed towards the end. I think that was the first time we did an interview with someone on a treadmill! Terry came on a few other times, but nothing compared to his first time on *Waddle and Silvy*.

Tony Dungy

    Tony Dungy is a Hall-of-Fame coach and a Hall-of-Fame person. I built a relationship with Coach Dungy going all the way back to his days as the Vikings' Defensive Coordinator since he was our playoff analyst at One-On-One Sports. When he got the job with the Bucs, he always came on our station and he always remembered our relationship. Before the biggest games, he was always available. I remember when I was working with Waddle and Silvy, I called his office the week of their big showdown against the Patriots. Both teams were undefeated. I didn't have high hopes that he would join us considering he had over 20 requests. However, on Friday morning, I was driving to a remote at a Cabela's sporting goods store in Indiana when Coach Dungy called my cell phone. He said he had a bunch of meetings, but he would try his best to come on. This was two days before the big game!

The story I will always remember is the Monday after the Colts beat the Bears in the Superbowl. I was producing *The James Brown Show* that morning from 10am-12pm central. JB and Coach Dungy were very tight, so I called Coach once the show started, but I assumed he had been up pretty late and maybe was asleep. Coach called me back around 12:15pm, right after JB ended his show. JB had been working the entire Super Bowl and CBS had the rights to the Super Bowl so, when he finished on Monday, he said "Randy, I'm going to sleep and not waking up for a week!" That meant to leave him alone.

When Coach called in, I congratulated him and said how happy I was for him. He thanked me and said, "Hey, is JB still on?" I said, "You just missed him, Coach. Any chance you can come on with our host who is on now?" He said, "Randy, I normally would, but today I will only go on with JB." I said, "Coach, give me a minute." I had to do it. I called JB in his hotel room. His wife, Dorothy, answered. She said, "Oh Randy, he's sound asleep." I said, "Dorothy, you have to wake him. Tony Dungy is on hold." She said, "Oh gosh. I will." Well, it took a few tries, but the big fella got up and came to the phone all groggy. I told him Coach Dungy was on hold and he could do the interview over the phone. He said, "Randy, give me five minutes." I said, "JB, the Coach who just won the Super Bowl has already been waiting for five minutes!" He cleared his head, threw some water on his face, and said, "Ok, I'm ready."

Then I witnessed one of the coolest moments of my career. He said, "Tony." Coach Dungy said, "Hey, JB I heard I woke you up." JB started crying. He kept saying, "I'm so proud of you." It was a very poignant moment. After a few more minutes, I don't know how JB did it, but he conducted a great interview. I think we ran it five times that day.

Twelve years later the Bears hosted the Packers to kick off the 2019 season. I texted Coach Dungy the Monday before the Thursday game and I asked if he would come on with Waddle and Silvy. He had built a good relationship with the guys. He said, "Of course!" I asked, "Any chance you can come in studio?" He said, "Assuming I get into town in time, yes." Well, on Wednesday he was scheduled to arrive at 3pm. He texted me that he didn't get to his hotel until 4:30. Most people would say let's just do it over the phone. Coach Dungy asked how far the studio was from his hotel. I told him probably a ten-minute cab ride or a twenty-minute walk. He responded, "I'm on my way." He literally dropped off his bags at the front desk and came right over and arrived at 4:55. I couldn't thank him enough. He responded, "It is always great to see you, Randy, and I love going on with the guys." That's why I do this job - because of guys like Tony Dungy!

John and Jim Harbaugh

John Harbaugh is a great coach of the Ravens. He is also very charismatic and a great interview. He was coaching the Pro Bowl in 2011. Calling the Pro Bowl hotel is always a blast since most players and coaches are listed and are always willing to come on and talk. I decided to call Coach Harbaugh and try to book him for the following day. Waddle and Silvy, at that time, were on from 9am-1pm and Tom was friends with Coach through his brother, Jim.

I called the hotel at 8am Hawaiian time. You have to call them early because that's the only time they are in their rooms. He was actually on his way out for a jog, but he told me to call him at 7am the following day and he would be glad to come on. I called the next day and his wife answered and said that Coach was on another jog. I told her that we had an interview set up. She gave me Coach

Harbaugh's cell phone and said feel free to call him. Coach didn't answer. Later that day, he called me back and apologized and asked if we could do something in the following weeks. That was fine with me.

A couple of weeks later, I reached out to Coach Harbaugh. He had a great suggestion. What if we put his brother on with him? I loved the idea. Now, the only problem was scheduling the interview. Jim Harbaugh had just accepted the position as the 9ers head coach and there was currently a lockout going on in the NFL. It was challenging to get the Harbaugh brothers on the same schedule. I went back and forth with both of them.

Finally, Coach John Harbaugh said he wanted to do the interview on Thursday at 11. He said, "Hopefully, Jim can join us." So I booked John for Thursday at 11. I texted Jim Harbaugh and asked if he was free. He responded right away that yes, he was, and he would be happy to join us. He gave me his office number in San Francisco. So, I finally had them on the line at once!

The interview was off to a great start. Both Harbaughs are engaging, thoughtful interviews. There was an incident in the Bears draft where they screwed over the Ravens when a trade was supposed to happen, but at last second, the Bears pulled out. The Ravens were not happy. Silvy asked John if what happened to the Bears would affect his dealings with the team going forward. I was expecting to hear a stock answer that it was no big deal. Instead, John Harbaugh spent the next two minutes absolutely destroying the Bears and Jerry Angelo. He said there is no way they would ever attempt to make a deal with the Bears again. We were all shocked. The guys did a great job with follow up questions and John wouldn't back down. It made huge news in Chicago. It was on the front page of the papers the following day. It was so scathing that Jerry Angelo reached out to Ozzie Newsome, General Manager of the Baltimore Ravens, to clear the air.

The interview was far from over. We heard great stories

about the Harbaughs growing up and how competitive they both were. We also talked about the possibility of them someday meeting in a Super Bowl, which they did two years later! At the end of the interview, Silvy asked both Harbaughs if either of them was interested in a 40-something broken down wide receiver to be their wide receiver coach. They both laughed and then both said they would love Waddle on their staff. It didn't happen!

While Jim was already a regular with Waddle and Silvy, this was the first time we had John Harbaugh on with the guys. It was clearly a memorable interview and one of the few times in which the guests helped make the interview better and assisted in setting it up.

Terrell Owens

Terrell Owens is a Hall-of-Fame wide receiver. He was also a Hall-of-Fame personality during his time in the NFL. There was no bigger story in 2005 than when TO and the Eagles parted ways. We all saw the scene of TO doing sit ups on his driveway. He was the guy to get, and everyone wanted to talk with TO. I had tried unsuccessfully in the past to book him, but I would continue to try!

I was producing weekends at Sporting News Radio. On this particular Saturday, Doug Russell and Bob Stelton were the hosts and our guest was the Senior NFL Writer from the Sporting News who was discussing his "sit down" with TO. He had spent a week with him, which included an interview at his house. He said that TO was quite the engaging subject and simply wanted to be heard.

With that in mind, I figured that I might as well give TO another shot. I had his home number in Atlanta. I didn't even tell Doug or Bob that I was trying him because I wasn't confident that he would say yes. I waited until the top of an hour to try him because that was the window when we had the most time. I called his house, and someone answered right away. I said, "TO?"

"No, this isn't TO. Who is this?"

"It's Randy with Sporting News Radio."

"What the f*** do you want?"

I told him that we were looking for a brief interview with TO. He asked how I got this number and I told him that I'd had it for a quite a while. He told me to hold on and then he screamed, "TO, it's for you."

Moments later, TO picked up the phone and asked, "Who is this?"

"It's Randy with Sporting News Radio."

He screamed, "How did you get my number?!"

I gave the same stock answer. He again asked what the hell I wanted. I said, "TO, you have to join my guys to tell your side of the story."

He yelled, "Why are you calling me at home?!"

I waited a second and responded, "TO, instead of yelling at me, why don't you come on the air and let the fans hear your side of the story?"

He paused and then screamed, "Put me on!"

I typed on the screen, "Go to TERRELL OWENS now!" I wish I could have taken a picture of Doug and Bob's reaction. Like the pros that they are, they transitioned right to TO. It started off a little rough, but he gave the guys fifteen great minutes and was very thoughtful with his answers. After the interview was over, I picked up the phone to thank him. He wasn't yelling anymore. He said, "No problem. Thanks for letting me tell my side of the story." He was always a blast to cover.

Mike Ditka

When I first started on *Waddle and Silvy*, one of the staples was *The Coach Ditka Show* every Thursday at noon. I had produced a ton of live shows with athletes and coaches but, for some reason, producing the show with Coach Ditka made me nervous. He was the Coach of my youth and the '85 Bears were everything to me! Now I was producing his show! My biggest mistake was not asking my predecessor, Danny Zederman, for tips on how to best produce this particular show.

The first show of the season we did with Coach Ditka was at his restaurant in Downtown Chicago. If you have ever been to this location for the show, you know it was always very cramped with many people who want to get a glimpse of the Coach. Whenever I produced a show like this, I would type out a bunch of topics for Waddle and Silvy, so they were prepared with questions for Coach. (Of course, they had their own topics and questions as well.) I always gave the same list to Coach before the show so he knew what to expect. He typically gave it a cursory glance and then started talking to the guys.

My first *Coach Ditka Show* got underway, and the first segment was very entertaining. Coach was engaged and gave thoughtful answers. During every break, there was usually a line of at least ten people wanting to get an autograph from Coach. He was always more than willing to sign for anyone, but he asked that they made a donation into his favorite charity, the Misericordia Home. He had a bucket for it next to him. The only problem with Coach signing autographs was that he sometimes would continue to sign far into the next segment. This wasn't ideal for the show because he was distracted.

There was a cut I wanted Coach to hear as we were coming back from break so that he could comment on it. It was really loud in the restaurant, so I waved my arms to get his attention and he was either ignoring me or didn't see me. He kept signing autographs! We were seconds away from playing the cut, so I went to grab his headphones for him to put on. It is worth mentioning that Coach always had a huge glass of iced tea in front of him that was never empty. In my haste to grab his headphones, I knocked the entire glass of iced tea in his lap! I immediately recognized the horror in this. All 120 people were staring at me. Jim Pastor, the General Manager of our station, was at the table adjacent to the stage and shook his head. Silvy gave me a dirty look. The only person that didn't seem to care was Coach Ditka! Four waiters and waitresses came running with napkins and began drying off his lap. I apologized profusely right away and then again at the break. He barely acknowledged me. I felt terrible about this situation.

Usually after the show, Tom would drive Silvy and me back to the station. Tom played for Coach Ditka for four years and knew him well. He told me not worry and that Coach would not hold a grudge the rest of the season and, most likely, he probably already forgot all about my knocking the tea into his lap. But I felt bad, so I made a donation to the Misericordia Home with a note apologizing again. Coach never acknowledged the donation or the note, but I never really expected him to.

There was another incident with Coach Ditka during the same season. They gave Coach a "live read" each week and there were two problems with that. The lighting wasn't great where we were set up at Ditka's downtown restaurant and Coach never really read it before he was live on the air. Each week, I would give it to him at the start of the show and remind him about it during each break. That didn't seem to matter! One week, as we went to break, I told Coach that his "read" would take place in a minute. He told me that he wasn't doing it! It was towards the end of the year and I think Coach was tired. Since the ambient noise was always very loud during the *Ditka Show*, I didn't think it was a problem when I complained to the producer back in the studio, "Coach is being difficult and won't do the read." Well, he heard me! He yelled back at me, "I'm being difficult?! Give me the f****** read!" He did and did it well. I didn't apologize and I almost think Coach respected me more for calling him out. Producing the *Ditka Shows* was fun, but each week was a new adventure!

Mike Singletary

Growing up a Bears fan, one of my favorite players from the 1985 Bears was Mike Singletary. I was in awe of him. He was such a great player and leader, but an even better person off the field. When I started in the sports radio business, I never thought that I would be the person to tell one of the greatest Bears linebackers of all time that he made the Hall of Fame.

It was the Saturday of Super Bowl week in 1998, which was one of my favorite days to produce. I loved having the opportunity to tell a great player that he made the Hall of Fame. This was long before the way they announce the Hall now. There wasn't the current fanfare, but someone in the selection room merely gave us the heads up who made it in. It was no surprise that Mike Singletary would make the Hall. As soon as I got the list, the first call I made was to Mike. He answered and I told him the good news! He was so excited and I asked him to come on. He said he would be happy to come on Sunday, but he wanted to spend Saturday with his family celebrating. I said that was no problem. I hung up and had the biggest grin on my face. I just told one of my favorite players that he was a Hall of Famer!

My other story involving Mike isn't as positive. He was the head coach of the 49ers. Not surprisingly, he had the same intensity as a coach that he did as a player. During a team meeting to get his point across, he may have gone too far. He dropped his pants to show his players how they were getting their asses whipped. It made big news in the NFL world. The following week, the 49ers had a bye week and I called him Monday morning to see if he would come on with Tom Waddle, since they were teammates on the Bears. It took a few minutes, but I convinced him to come on. I was all set to call him back in 20 minutes. True to his word, he came on with Waddle and Silvy. It was an uncomfortable interview, but Waddle and Silvy did a good job handling it. After the interview was done, I was surprised with the attention it drew. Cuts were played on ESPN throughout the rest of the week. I felt bad for Mike Singletary. He wanted to make his mark as a head coach, but I'm sure this attention wasn't what he was looking for.

Bill Parcells

Bill Parcells is one of the most intimidating people I have ever dealt with. Whether it was trying to book him as a guest or producing his radio show, I was always a little afraid of him. Back in the day, One-On-One Sports was sold to Paul Allen, who also owned the Sporting News. So we now had new teammates on the radio side. We worked hand in hand in making sure we were on the same page with what we were always reporting. One Saturday morning, I was producing in studio when I got a call from the assignment desk in St. Louis, where their offices were. They were reporting that Bill Parcells was taking the Cowboys job. I said, "Excuse me?!" At the time, Coach Parcells was working with us hosting his own show with Bruce Murray. They told me, "You guys should go with the story. We are putting it up right now." I asked if they were 100 percent confident in this story and they said they were. So we went with it. I called our NFL insider, Bob Glauber, and told him the news. He covered Coach Parcells when he was with the Jets and Giants. He called Coach Parcells, who at the time was doing work for ESPN during the playoffs, and he told Bob it wasn't true and to leave him alone! Around an hour later, Sporting News assignment desk called me back and said they were backing off the story. "What?! Really?! We are reporting it!" They said, "Well, you can continue to report it." I was not happy.

I had an idea. Bruce Murray, who was the co-host of the show, was on vacation. Bruce was always on vacation! I said to Bob Berger, "What if we put Bruce on to get his thoughts on this potential move? After he's done, let's have him call Coach and do an interview with him over the phone." This was before texting was a thing.

So, I called Bruce and explained to him what I was looking for. He said, "You do know Coach will not be happy with me." I said, "He loves working with you. Call him." He called me back twenty minutes later and said, "All right. He said to call him in his hotel in thirty minutes." Bruce gave me his room number and I went down to the other studio. Even though the interview was already set up, I was still nervous to call him. I asked for his room and Coach answered right away. I said, "Hey Coach it's Randy with Bruce." He said, "Hi ya, Randy. Hold on a minute." He was watching the Fox Pre-Game Show. They were talking about him taking the Cowboys job and he was screaming at the TV. I heard him say, "Ah that's not right." He then told me, "All right. Go ahead, Randy." Bruce and Coach did a great 7-minute interview. Bruce's final question of Coach was, "My wife, Hilary, likes expensive things. Can I tell her that she's ok to keep buying them?" He said, "Tell her to buy away." We ran the interview a couple of times that day. I think less than a week later, Bill Parcells was the new head coach of the Cowboys. That's how it works. You have to protect yourself and make sure all the i's are dotted and the t's are crossed.

A side note story on Bill Parcells. We taped the *Bill Parcells Show* every week on Wednesday to run on Thursday. Each week, we would replace the old show in our system. However, one week the old show wasn't purged correctly. I remember it like it was yesterday. I was standing in the studio and I knew exactly how the show started. I heard the first 10 seconds and I screamed, "We are running last week's show." Lonnie Willems, who was running the board, asked what we should do. I said, "Call master control and try to get this week's show in the system ASAP." I then went running into our PD Mark Gentzkow's office and announced, "Mark, we are running the wrong Parcells show!" Before he could say anything, over the intercom we heard, "Mark, Bill Parcells is on hold." He went white. He said, "All right, Randy, go pick up the phone and tell Coach we are on it."

"You want me to talk to him? Isn't that your job?"

"I have got to get the right show on the air."

By the time I got to the phone, he had hung up. Turns out that the Bears GM, Jerry Angelo, was an avid listener. When he heard the wrong show, he called Bill Parcells and told him. We did get the right show on the air and explained the mistake to Coach. Mark, the Program Director, was so pissed he called a 4am meeting the next morning!

NFL Draft

The NFL Draft is one of my least favorite events to produce. I would stand for eight hours on a Saturday in a cramped row with people all around me. This was before laptops were common. I would produce with note cards and a stopwatch and I relied on the producer back in the studio for information about an upcoming draft pick or anything else pertinent.

There are two stories that stick with me regarding the draft. It was always held at Madison Square Garden and our location was always bad. They stuck us way high up, which wasn't great when it came to getting the draft choices to stop by our area. That was ok with me. It just meant I had to hustle a little more. However, one year the NFL asked our network to carry a few NFL Europe games for them. They promised that if we did, one of the perks would be a great spot for the draft. Well, we did and they did! We were literally set up a row above the Pittsburgh Steelers draft set up which, for a minute, I thought could potentially be a problem. Before we even started at noon, one of the Steelers draft guys turned to me and said, "You have to move. You are too close to us."

"Where do you want me go?"

"Anywhere but here."

I moved as far away from him as possible. The next issue was that I was being too loud. He turned around and said to me, "Please be quiet." Again, I apologized and told him I would try. (By the way, I could see their draft board and saw who they wrote down on their card for their picks.)

Our show started. It was Bob Berger, Bob Stelton and Brian Baldinger. Baldy played in the NFL for over ten years. He is probably 6' 3" and 275 pounds and all muscle. The guys were breaking down the first pick. Then we went to break. The Steelers draft guy stood up and said to Bob Berger, "Shut up." Bob responded, "We are doing a radio show. There's not much we can do." He shouted, "Well, if you don't shut up, I will come up there and do it myself." Bob Berger shrugged and urged him to come on up. The guy jumped up and started heading up. Bob Stelton noticed what was going on. A little background on Bob Stelton -- he is an accomplished boxer and a really strong guy. Bob jumped up and got ready. Then Baldy, who can be rather intimidating, saw the guy coming up and stood up. He said to the Steelers representative, "Do we have a problem here? Come on, really? Do you have an issue with us? Why don't you go sit down?" He did sit down and did not bug us the rest of the draft!

The second draft story took place on day two. It was Wayne Gretzky's final game in the NHL. He was playing for the Rangers and both events were being held at the Garden. Bob Berger, Bruce Murray and Tim Parker called me up at 8:30am and said they were going for breakfast. I told them I was going to work out. Tim had my credential and I asked him to leave it for me at the front desk. I went down at 9:45am. We were starting the day at noon and it took half an hour to get from our hotel to walk to the Garden. Well, the front desk had no envelope for me! This was the late 90's and there were no cell phones! So, I sprinted over to the Garden. I begged them to let me in. No dice. I ran across the street where I had to wait to use the pay phone. Then I called our 800 number and told them to have Tim Parker come meet me with my credential! They said they would try. An hour later, Tim came with my credential. He was furious with me, as were Bob and Bruce. I was pretty pissed at them as well. Anyways, I got there after the show started. An hour in and we were back to normal. But for a short time, I thought I wasn't going to be able to produce the show. That was just another fun adventure!

Troy Aikman

Back when I was working at Sporting News Radio, I had the great opportunity to produce the *Troy Aikman Show*. Troy was great to work with since he put a lot of work into his show each week. The host for the first two years was my good friend, Bruce Murray. After Bruce left the network, the Cowboys play-by-play voice, Brad Sham, took over. Each week, I would touch base with the guys on Tuesday with some notes for the show. We usually taped on Thursday around 1 or 2pm. I would ask Troy each week if he wanted me to try for a guest. In my three years of producing the show, I believe Tom Brady was the only QB to turn Troy down. I usually tried to get the biggest name QB from the top game of that week. Well, back in 2006, the Cowboys were facing off against the Eagles. It was the first time Donovan McNabb would face his old teammate Terrell Owens. Things did not end well between the two of them. I reached out to the Eagles and requested that Donovan join Troy's show. Outside of his Fox commitments, he wasn't doing any interviews. However, he agreed to talk with Troy. I was psyched!

That Tuesday, I sent over questions to Brad and Troy. Usually, before the show we would chat for about twenty minutes to go over topics and questions for the guest. They said, "Hey, we got your questions for Donovan, but we are not going to ask anything about TO." I was shocked. I said, "Guys, the whole point to this interview is the TO questions." We went back and forth for like five minutes. I said, "Troy, the reason why Donovan agreed to this interview is because he knows you will be fair and ask the right questions." They finally agreed to ask two questions at the end. The logistics of the show were that Troy and Brad did the show from a studio in Dallas. This particular week we had a new engineer on their end. We had issues connecting, but finally got it set up. We started taping the McNabb interview and it was going well. We only had about seven minutes with him. We were now five in and still no TO questions. Our Program Director, Matt Nahigian, walked in and asked how it was going. I turned around and said, "It would be much better if they would ask a question about TO." A second later, the phone rang in the studio. It was the engineer from Dallas. He said, "Hey, I don't know how, but they can hear you. They aren't happy!" I asked how that was possible. He said, "I must have wired something wrong." Anyways, Troy and Brad ended up asking two great questions on TO. After the interview ended, Troy and Brad asked if Donovan was off the line. They went off on me! I deserved it, so I took the yelling. However, I did tell them that I was just as concerned as they were about the show. I did apologize to Brad and Troy and, to their credit, they moved on. Our relationship was fine for the rest of the year. It taught me to be careful of a hot mic!

John Elway

John Elway is one of the best quarterbacks to ever play the game of football. I always wanted to book John because, in my eyes, he was almost larger than life. In the late 90's, when I was just starting to hit my sweet spot as a producer, calling hotels was a very common way to book a big-name guest. John Elway rarely listed himself. Back in the pre-season of 1997, the Broncos had a great team. They were playing their third pre- season game on Saturday night. The third game is usually when the starters used to play most of the game. I figured, why not call John Elway in the hotel? The worst that could happen is he would decline the interview. It took me a while, but I found where the Broncos were staying, and he was listed! I asked for his room and he answered right away. He asked how I got his room number and I told him that he was listed. He chuckled and I asked if he could join us for like three minutes. My heart was beating so fast. He said, "Sure, go ahead." I typed so fast on the screen GO TO JOHN ELWAY NOW. To see Bob and Bruce's reaction was priceless. He spent more than three minutes with us and was a great guest. After the interview, I picked up the phone to thank him and he was really nice. I had a huge sense of accomplishment after booking John Elway.

The following year it was the same scenario - the third pre-season game on the road. I called John again in his hotel room. I reminded him that we did the same thing last year. He remembered and said, "Go ahead and put me on again, but this is the last time. Ok?" He was sending me a message! He won back-to-back Super Bowls and retired after the '98 season.

We got the news on a Sports Saturday show when John Elway retired. The guest to get, outside of Elway and Mike Shanahan, was Bubby Brister. Yes, I said Bubby Brister. He was the heir apparent to take over for one of the greatest quarterbacks of all time. How do I get Bubby Brister's number? Well, I looked up where he was from and I found his parents' house and called them. They were very nice and gave me Bubby's number. I called him right away and he was also a super nice guy. He said, "Give me an hour and I will be happy to come on." I waited an hour and called back. He was ready to go. It's crazy to say getting Bubby Brister was a huge get that day!

One more Elway story. My best friend from college, Eric Newmark aka Newmy, is the biggest Broncos fan I know. He always told me that Gary Kubiak was better than Elway. I know he was just being a putz, but he said it over and over again. I think it was the 2002 Super Bowl and John Elway was joining us on the set because he was promoting the AFL. He sat down during the break. We had five minutes before we came back, and I had to tell him Newmy's crazy statement. I said, "John, my roommate from college believes that Gary Kubiak was better than you!" He smiled and said, "Did he graduate?" Great line!

Andy Reid

One of the legendary coaches in football, Andy Reid is also a quality individual. I never had a bad experience with Coach Reid. In 2004, Andy Reid kicked Simeon Rice out of the Pro Bowl! Who gets kicked out of the Pro Bowl? Well, I called Andy in his hotel that night and he couldn't have been more accommodating. He came on with Chet Coppock and gave us his reasons why he sent Simeon home.

Fast forward a few years. The Chiefs were in the Super Bowl and I found out before the game where they were staying. Andy Reid, back in the day, coached Jurko! That was my in. If the Chiefs won, I was calling Andy Reid in his hotel. Well, the Chiefs beat the 9ers. Monday morning at 9:20 I called the Chiefs hotel and asked for Coach Reid's room. They said he had a block on his phone. I asked them to tell Coach that Jurko was on the line. Literally five seconds later, I heard on the other line "JURKO!!!" I said, "Coach, it's actually Randy Merkin, Jurko's producer, congratulations!" I said, "Hey, do you have time this morning to join Jurko's show?" He said, "Of course. Can we do it now?" I said, "Actually, Jurko won't be in for another hour." He told me that they are leaving in ten minutes. "I tell you what. I promise I will come on this week. Just email our PR guy. I will let him know I want to do the interview. I will do this interview with Jurko." Pretty crazy - the guy just won the biggest game of his life and he's committed to coming on our station.

So, I emailed the PR guy and, three days later, Coach Reid was on with Carmen and Jurko. The only reason he came on that week was for Jurko, but if I hadn't reached out to him, we would never have had him on. In May of 2020, I texted Coach Reid again and asked if he would come on with Jurko. He responded right away again and said of course. I went through the Chiefs' PR staff and Coach came on with Carmen and Jurko for fifteen minutes. To have the ability to interview the Super Bowl-winning coach on your show more than once in a calendar year is remarkable. I asked

Coach for his address and sent him some Lou's pizza and some cookies. He sent me a text after he received the pizza that he loved it and will always come on for Jurko! Sometimes after you have a guest on, especially a big- name guest like Coach Reid, it helps to do more than just send a thank you text. It goes a long way!

Kurt Warner

No one has had a better story than Kurt Warner. He went from bagging groceries to being a two-time MVP and Hall of Famer. The one thing about Kurt Warner is he never changed who he was. He is one of the nicest superstars I have ever dealt with. Here are a couple of stories that exemplify Kurt's character.

Back in 1999, when Kurt Warner took over for Trent Green, the Rams became the best story in the NFL. Everyone wanted to talk with Kurt. I was producing a show called *Around the NFL*. I used to hire stringers for each game to do reports and book guests after the game. Usually, they would get one of the bigger stars from the game. After Kurt Warner's first home game, I asked our stringer to ask Kurt to call in. He did - maybe an hour after the game. After each ensuing win, I would make the same request. And, after each win, Kurt called in. He always called in the same way and said the same thing, "Hey, it's Kurt Warner, the quarterback of the Rams. I was asked to call in." No matter how big Kurt got, he always stayed humble. Even on the road, I would have our stringer approach him after the game and he remembered who we were and always came on.

Back in 2001, I was blessed with the opportunity to do shows from the Pro Bowl and we broadcasted from the NFC and AFC practices. The NFL media told me one thing... "You have around thirty minutes after each practice to grab whoever you want. However, if you are waiting for a big star, like Peyton Manning or Kurt Warner, you might not get anyone." They usually spent thirty minutes signing autographs for the fans who were there.

It was the day of the NFC practice. Once practice ended, I sprang into action. I grabbed two pro bowlers right away and brought them on stage with Bob Berger, Bruce Murray, Brian Baldinger and Paul Attner from the Sporting News. I had my eye on Kurt Warner, but he was signing every autograph. I turned around for one second and he was gone. I sprinted into the locker room to find him and he was already changed. I said, "Kurt, any chance you have like five minutes to join us on the field?"

"I wish I could, but I have to jump on a bus. We are headed to the local hospital to meet with some sick kids."

"No problem. I understand."

I went back onstage and told the guys that it was no go on Kurt.

We were in our next segment when I felt a tap on my shoulder. It was Kurt Warner. He said, "I arranged for a ride. I have like 20 minutes. Does that work?"

"Absolutely!"

As I stated before, he is one of the nicest superstars you will ever meet.

Side note - I was at a Super Bowl party a year later with some of my colleagues. I saw Kurt Warner and his wife Brenda just kind of hanging out. I approached him and re-introduced myself. Not surprisingly, he was super friendly. I even took a picture with him!

Bart Starr

Bart Starr is a legendary QB and a wonderful man. I booked him a few times to celebrate Packer anniversaries. However, I had never met him. I was working the '99 Super Bowl in Atlanta. Our boss, Mark Gentzkow, had set up a work room for us in the hotel where we were broadcasting. This place was huge like a ballroom! They brought food in all day long and there were tons of beverages to pick from. I'm really not sure why he did it, but thanks, Mark.

Anyways, we would have to take an escalator up to our broadcast position on Radio Row. I was walking down the hallway on

Thursday and noticed that NFLPA had set up a room right across the hall from us. I had my eye on that room. I saw some players walk in and out, but I didn't notice anyone big. Then it happened. I was walking by on Thursday afternoon and I saw Bart Starr in the room signing footballs. There must have been 250 footballs in there! Here was my chance. He was sitting by himself in the room. I went in and introduced myself. He was very cordial. I said, "It looks like you are very busy, but do you possibly have time later to come up to our site to join us?"

"Which station, Randy?"

I told him it was One-On-One Sports. He said, "Sure. I listen often. I'm going to take a pass, Randy. As you can see, I have a ton of footballs to sign, and I don't want to get stuck doing a bunch of interviews up there." I said, "Mr. Starr, I understand, but this would mean the world to our network. We are located right by the elevators. We can do the interview and I can have security walk you right to the elevators."

"How about this? Check back with me in an hour." I told him I would. I waited an hour and went back in. He said, "I'm sorry, Randy, I just don't see it happening."

"How about we wait one more hour? Can we do that?"

He chuckled and said, "Sure, one more hour."

I was nervous. This was probably my only chance to have Bart Starr on in person. I went back in an hour later. He was sitting in his chair and had finished signing all of the footballs. He looked at me and said, "You promise after I'm done with you guys, you can get me out with no issue?"

"It's already set up." I had spoken to a security guard on Radio Row and told him my situation. He said he would be happy to help.

"Ok, let's do it!"

It was so cool walking with Bart. He was such a nice man and told me a few stories on our way. I felt like a proud papa going up the escalator with him and walking him to our set! Sometimes persistence pays off!

Brandon Marshall

Brandon Marshall and Jay Cutler were always tied together, which comes from their time together in Denver. They were just starting out in their careers and were a great duo, but then Jay Cutler was traded to the Bears. I remember watching the Lions vs Saints playoff game. Matthew Stafford and Calvin Johnson went off. Jay Cutler and Brandon Marshall were tweeting at each other that night saying, "We should get the band back together." That same year, Brandon Marshall made the Pro Bowl. I loved calling the Pro Bowl hotel because you will never find friendlier hotel operators than at the Aulani Hotel in Hawaii, where they always answered the phone with a cheerful "Aloha."

Honolulu was four hours behind. I went on the Pro Bowl schedule to find out the practice schedule for the AFC. Back then, Waddle and Silvy were on from 9am-1pm. I only had about an hour window to call players. I found the day that the AFC was practicing at 9am, so I called Brandon Marshall at 7:45am his time, 11:45am our time. He answered on the first ring. I said, "Brandon, it's Randy with ESPN 1000. How are you?

"Good."

"Do you have like five minutes for us right now?"

"What??"

"Can you do a phone interview right now with us?"

"For real?"

"Yes, it would be real quick."

"Sure, go ahead. Hey, how did you get my room number?"

I told him that his name was listed! He responded, "Ah, I didn't know that."

I generally give the hosts a "heads up" when I am trying guests on the fly in a hotel. So, I put Brandon on with Silvy and JD, who was filling in for Waddle that day. The guys did a great job and Brandon Marshall is an outstanding interview. The guys had a great conversation going when Silvy asked him about his tweets with Jay

Cutler. Silvy said, "Brandon, why don't you get the band back together?" He seemed intrigued! Anyways, they let Brandon go after around an 8-minute interview. I don't think most producers realized how great the Pro Bowl hotel is. Almost every big-name NFL Player and Coach are listed. It's a goldmine!

Just over a month later, we get breaking news. Brandon Marshall was now a Chicago Bear!! Holy cow! We figured we are going to the Super Bowl. Over the next couple of years, we started *The Jay Cutler Show*. It was an in-person show at various bars. It was a huge success and always had a gigantic crowd. One week, Brandon was filling in for Jay. During the show, he told Waddle and Silvy that our interview with him at the Pro Bowl was the impetus for his asking to be traded to the Bears. He wasn't kidding! It was a very cool moment for us. Brandon became a good friend to *The Waddle and Silvy Show*. In all my dealings with Brandon, he was always great.

Tim Dwight and Jeff Garcia

You might wonder what these two NFL players have in common. Back in the day, when I was working at One-On-One Sports, we had a deal with the NFLPA. We ran their weekend program for an hour on Saturday night each week during the NFL season. Our reward was being the exclusive radio show at their two big parties Super Bowl week. So, we were doing our show on a Tuesday night from an Air Force Base in Tampa. The crowd was huge and it was chaotic. I was dealing with my good friend Doug Finniff from the NFLPA. He was helping me bring by at least two players each hour to join Bob Berger and Bruce Murray. Matt Nahigian, my colleague, was also there bringing players over. Here's the thing about NFL players - they are always wearing a helmet, and when they are not, it's sometimes tough to determine who they are. That's why I had always had a sharpie and a bunch of note cards. As soon as I knew who was coming next, I would write it out and put it in front of Bob and Bruce.

Well, Doug came up to me during the break and suggested, "How about Tim Dwight from the Falcons? He just had a great year." I told him that worked. He said, "Ok, I will go grab him." I told Bob and Bruce to expect Tim Dwight during the next segment. Meanwhile, Matt Nahigian came up to me and said, "Hey, I just saw Jeff Garcia, do you want him?" I said, "Absolutely, I will take the starting QB from the 49ers." We went to break, and I went to get something to drink and, when I got back, Bob and Bruce were on the air. I turned around for one second and there was a player sitting right across from Bob and Bruce. I just assumed it was Tim Dwight because that was who Doug said he was getting. Matt had indicated that it would take a while to bring Jeff Garcia over. Bruce assumed the same thing said, "Joining us now from the players party is Tim Dwight. Tim how are ya?"

The player responded, "Tim Dwight? I'm Jeff Garcia."

Bruce chuckled and said, "My bad. There's a lot going on behind the scenes." Not surprising, Bruce handled it like a pro. I was horrified for a second, but everyone involved just laughed it off. Jeff was an outstanding interview. I was curious how Bruce would handle it when we went to break. He just looked at me and said, "Well, that's one we will remember." We never did get Tim Dwight!

Johnny Unitas

I never got to see Johnny Unitas play, but I've heard he was one of the all-time greats! I also knew he had an affinity for the horses. When I worked at One-On-One Sports, we went to the Kentucky Derby three straight years to do our shows. I produced Bob and Bruce's show on Saturday. Friday morning we would get up at 5am and head to the backstretch to interview the trainers. They couldn't stand us. We knew nothing about horse racing, and they knew it! However, it was our job, so we pushed through. The cool part about being on the backstretch is that we had amazing access and a great look at the behind-the-scenes of the biggest event in horse racing. It was also a huge attraction for celebrities and athletes. During my years on the backstretch, I saw the likes of Bo Derek, Paul Hornung, Dick Vitale and many more celebrities. Most were very approachable and friendly.

We were wrapping up our interviews one Friday when I saw Johnny Unitas. I said to Bob and Bruce, "Hey, there is Johnny U. Let's go interview him." They both said that he doesn't look like he wants to be bothered. He was surrounded by a few people. I said, "This is the whole reason we are here!" So I decided to break the ice and approach the Hall of Fame QB. I went up to him and said, "Mr. Unitas, how are you? I'm Randy Merkin with One-On- Sports." He just shook his head. I asked, "Is there any chance you might have like three minutes to tape an interview with our hosts?"

"About what?"

"About football, life and horses."

He looked right into my eyes and said, "I loved playing football. Life is good and horses run fast." He then turned around and walked away from me. I chuckled. As I walked back to Bob and Bruce they said, "I'm assuming that's a no?"

"Oh yeah, that's a no." I'm actually happy he said no. It makes for a better memory!

COLLEGE FOOTBALL

Jim Harbaugh

The former great Bears QB Jim Harbaugh has now become one of the best coaches in college football. He is also Tom Waddle's former teammate and good friend. Nearly four years ago, we had a planning meeting for our show called *Lunch with a Legend*. They told me we needed to "up our game" as far as Legends went. I gave them a list of top tier legends and Jim Harbaugh was on top of it. I reached out to Michigan Sports Information and asked if we could possibly do a show when Coach Harbaugh was in town for Big Ten Media day. They said they would ask Coach. The initial response was that he was just too busy during the week. However, Zach Eisendrath, who was the Michigan Sports Information Director, told me to give him another chance. I think I caught him at a bad time.

Here is a little back story between me and Coach Harbaugh... I would not say we were friends, but I would say I was more of a pest for Coach! I sent him many texts saying, "Tom wants to know if you can join his show?" He usually responded to around every 5th text. A week later, I got a text from Zach that said Coach was available. We worked out all the details and were all set.

Now we were prepared for Coach to arrive at 1pm. He pulled up in the SUV we provided for him and emerged with his wife and three of his kids. I approached him and said, "Hey Coach! Randy Merkin, nice to finally meet you." He pulled out his phone and said, "Randy Merkin! You know how many times I have received a text from Randy Merkin?!"

"Sorry about that."

"I love it!"

We were holding the show at the downstairs banquet hall at Chicago Cut restaurant. We went down the escalator talking about his recent trip to Tahoe to play in the celebrity golf event. I asked if he was ok to take some pictures with big Michigan fans before going on with Waddle and Silvy. He said, "Absolutely, lead the way." That lasted for nearly thirty minutes. Then, I walked him up on the stage in front of a sold-out crowd to greet his friend and former teammate, Tom Waddle. It was an amazing commercial- free hour. Waddle and Silvy hit all the big topics with Coach Harbaugh. When they were letting him go, he said how much fun he had. He then pulled out his phone and said, "Next time Randy texts me, I will answer and come on." He said, "Where is Randy? Randy, you do know I have another job, right??" Waddle was saying goodbye to him and Coach said, "Waddle, can I get a hug??" They embraced for like five seconds! After the show, I asked Tom what he said to him. He said, "Coach told me he missed me and loves me. I said the same." This is a special friendship. After the show was done, Coach wasn't finished. He went upstairs and signed footballs for us and recorded a message for Coach Ditka, who was being honored by Pittsburgh. It was a great day that I will never forget! By the way, I still bug Coach Harbaugh!

John David Washington

John David Washington is a great young actor and his dad, Denzel Washington, happens to be pretty successful as well! John was a senior at Morehouse College when news came out that he was signing a free agent deal with the St Louis Rams. At the time, I was working at Sporting News Radio. I thought, What better guest then Denzel's son?

I reached out to Morehouse College Sports Information and asked for his cell phone number. They were great and gave it to me. I called John, but he didn't answer. I tried back a few more times over the next hour and he finally answered. He said he would be happy to come on, but he was studying for finals. He asked if we could we do it tomorrow and I told him that we were just looking for five minutes.

"Ok, go ahead and do it now then."

I put him on with Tony Bruno. John was great! He was so respectful of Tony and his co-host Mark Willard. I remember really liking John. Tony asked him which, of all of Denzel's films was his favorite. John said The Preacher's Wife with Whitney Houston. Tony asked, "It wasn't Training Day?" John laughed and said, "No, it was too violent." Then Tony kept saying throughout the rest of the interview that "King Kong ain't got nothing on me!" John thought it was funny the first time, but by the fifth time, I think he had enough. I felt bad that we were now keeping him from his studies. I told the guys to let him go. John David Washington didn't have much of a career with the Rams, but he has gone on to be a great actor like his dad.

Dabo Swinney

Dabo is one of the best coaches in College Football and also one of the best interviews. The first time they beat Bama in the title game, it was my goal to get him on the air. I reached out to my friend, Craig Larson, who runs Sports Map Radio and asked if he had his number. He did! I texted Dabo the day after he won. I was shocked that he got right back to me. He said there was probably no way he could do anything that week, but to touch back with him the following week. We played text tag over the next couple of weeks.

The life of a college coach is crazy. He was already back on the road recruiting, but we finally found a time for him to come on with David Kaplan. He was outstanding! It was the year when the Bears had the third pick. He told Kap that Deshaun Watson was Michael Jordan and that the Bears should draft him. I wish Ryan Pace would have listened. Fast forward three years and Dabo was in Chicago. He was tweeting from a bunch of different venues. I texted and asked him to come on, but he said he was with his boys and was just too busy. I saw that he tweeted out the next day that he was at Wrigley with his boys before he left Chicago. I texted him again.

"Hey, I'm sitting 4 rows behind home plate, so if you don't mind the noise, I can do it right now."

We had five minutes left in the show. I put him on with Carmen and Jurko. He was great! He told some great stories about his life, spending time with his family and Deshaun Watson. It couldn't have worked out better. This is another example of persistence paying off!

Tim Tebow

Tim Tebow will go down as one of the best players in college football history. He is also one of the nicest athletes I have ever dealt with. I have two stories about Tim. The first goes back to the championship against Ohio St. when Florida destroyed Ohio St. Chris Leak was the offensive player of the game. The next morning, I found the hotel where they were staying at and I called Chris Leak's room. Someone answered and I said, "Chris?"

"No, he's downstairs doing media."

"Who is this?"

He told me it was Tim. "Tim Tebow?" I asked. He said it was. He was a freshman and scored two touchdowns in the title game.

"Hey, would you have a few minutes to join us on Sporting News Radio?"

"For sure. I would be happy to".

It was a great interview that lasted about five minutes. Now, fast forward to 2011. One of my favorite annual events is to call athletes and celebrities at is the American Century Celebrity Championship, which takes place at Tahoe. The top name players and celebs play this event every year and the best part is they are always listed. I got the tee times for all the players that day. They usually go down an hour before their tee time to hit the range. Tim Tebow's tee time was 12:40 central, so I called him at 10 central, which is 8 Tahoe time. I figured he would be up early. He answered on the first ring. I said, "Tim, it's Randy with ESPN 1000. How are you?"

"Great!"

I asked if he had five minutes for us before he hit the course.

"You know what? I'm going down to have breakfast with my agent. If you call back in an hour, I will make sure I am back upstairs and be happy to do the interview."

Usually, when an athlete says that, he is giving you the Heisman. I gave Waddle and Silvy a heads up but assumed Tim Tebow wouldn't be there.

I called the hotel at 11 and asked for Tim's room. One the first ring, not only did he answer, but he said "Hey, Randy, I'm all ready to go." I thought that was very cool and classy. Of course, it was another great interview. Some athletes don't live up to the hype or aren't as nice as their image. Tim Tebow is the real deal!

AJ McCarron

AJ McCarron is the fine QB from Bama. I watched them as they won yet another championship. He has always been a great interview and I had a cell number for AJ, but he hadn't responded in a while. The night of the championship, I found the hotel where they were staying. The next day I called the hotel and someone answered. I asked if it was AJ and he said, "No, it's Barrett." Barrett was the stud Offensive Lineman, Barrett Jones.

I asked if AJ was around and he said, "No man, he already left he had to do a bunch of media."

"Got yah, can you confirm that this is his current cell

"Sure- go for it."

I gave him the cell and he said, "Nope, that's no longer it."

"Could give me his new one?" At first he said no, but eventually he gave it to me and told me not to bug him.

I texted AJ and he got back to me right away. He said he would be happy to come on, but asked if I could go through the Bama SID. I said, " AJ, if I do that, I might not get you on before the next football season. Any chance I can call you right now?" He said, "Go ahead."

I put him on with Waddle and Silvy. He was outstanding. At that time he was dating Katherine Webb and during the game they kept focusing on her. Brent Musburger was obsessed with Katherine. We asked AJ if he had heard the clip. He said he had not, so we played it for him and I remember he responded, "Take it easy, Brent." Those are always the best guests to have on - the big-name guest the day after a big game. AJ was awesome! I'm so glad he agreed to come on.

GOLF

Tom Watson

Tom Watson is a legend in the game of golf, and I have booked him in the past. I remember calling him after one of his rounds in the Open Championship. He hadn't played great, but it was still Tom Watson. He wasn't thrilled that I called him in the hotel. That's a preamble for what happened in 2009...

Tom Watson was 59 years old and was in the field at the Open. He shot a first round 4 under par and was tied for the lead. He played really early and was done by 10am central time. I found the hotel where the golfers were staying and thought it would be cool to have one of the leaders from the Open on with Waddle and Silvy. Also, it was an extra incentive to have Tom Watson!

I let the guys know I was going to try Tom. I remember being a little nervous considering that the last time I called him, he chewed me out, but he still did the interview. I asked for his room and he answered on the first ring. I said, "Tom, it's Randy with ESPN 1000. Congratulations on a great round."

"Not bad for an old guy, right?"

"Not bad at all. Any chance you have five minutes for us?"

He said that he would be happy to do it. I think the guys were kind of shocked that he was coming on, but he went on for about seven minutes and was totally engaging. I was really excited since I'm a golf nut and thought it was so awesome to have Tom on live after his first round.

Fast forward now to the Monday after the Open. Tom played his butt off all weekend. He had a 12-foot putt to win the Open that, unfortunately, he left woefully short. He lost in the playoff to Stewart Cink. Just to clarify, if Tom Watson had won the Open, it would have gone down as a top five sports accomplishments ever!

During the final round I heard that Tom was playing in the Senior Open and was leaving right after his final round. I looked up where the Seniors were playing and found the hotel where he was staying. I thought, "Boy if I can get Tom to come on again, that would be incredible." He had not done any radio interviews yet. It was now JD and Waddle hosting and I let them know that I was going to try Tom. I called him around 1pm central. He answered again on the first ring. I could already tell he was not as friendly as the last time. I said, "Tom, it's Randy again with ESPN 1000. Congratulations on an amazing run." He answered, "Thanks. I'm not a big fan of you calling me in my room." I told him that I understood and asked him if he had five minutes to spare. He said, "Go ahead, put me on." The first four minutes were great, with him talking about the agony of losing and the emotions he felt. Then, unfortunately, his phone went bad. We had to end the interview early. I believe that was the only radio interview he did that day. It was very special to have Tom Watson on twice within a calendar week during that amazing 2009 Open.

Dustin Johnson

One of the best golfers in the world, Dustin Johnson, is like Greg Norman in many ways. He was an amazing talent but could never win the Major. He was in contention at the PGA Championship at Whistling Straits. The Final round was between DJ, Bubba Watson, and Martin Kaymer. I thought, "This could be a crazy final round. I'm going to find where these guys are staying and try to get their cell phones so I could call them on Monday if they win." No one ever answered in Kaymer or Bubba's room, but I did speak with DJ's girlfriend. She told me that I just missed DJ. I explained to her that I was trying to get in touch with DJ just in case he won on Monday. She thought that was great planning and she was kind enough to give me his cell phone. I thanked her and settled in to watch the golf.

I was right - it was a crazy final round. DJ's tee shot on 18 ended up in a sandy area, which was not designated as a sand trap. DJ grounded his club in the sand. He ended up making a par. When he finished, a rules official informed him that he had grounded his club in a sand trap and would be assessed a 2-stroke penalty. He was in shock since he just missed the playoff. Martin Kaymer won, but the story was DJ getting screwed. Guess who had his cell phone? I called DJ during the *Waddle and Silvy Show* and asked if he would come on. He said he would, but asked if I would give him an hour. I thought he potentially was going to blow me off. However, an hour later, he answered and came on. I believe we were the only station to speak with him! I remember Silvy asked him point blank, "Dustin, do you think you got screwed? Did the PGA let you down?" He point blank said they did. It was the money quote! Within the hour it was on *Sportscenter* and then it was picked up everywhere. I kept thinking, "Man, a little extra work on Sunday morning led to a home-run guest on Monday." It was a great golf guest, and it wasn't Tiger.

Brooks Koepka

One of the top golfers in the world is Brooks Koepka. Unfortunately, most of the elite golfers are not available very often for radio interviews. Brooks was red hot, winning back-to-back US Opens and PGA Championships.

In 2018 Carmen and Jurko were doing their show from Conway Farms in Lake Forest, where the top players were playing during the Fed Ex Cup playoff. We had a great location. Carmen and Jurko were set up right by the players' entrance into their lounge and hospitality area. We saw Jordan Spieth, Matt Kuchar, Rickie Fowler, Rory McIlroy, and others walking right by us. During one of our first breaks, an ice cream company, which was set up right by us, came over with some ice cream cups for us. That was huge since I was starving! I polished off two chocolate ice cream cups in less than half an hour. The only problem is you had to use those little wooden spoons and they don't work very well.

We were in the middle of another segment and Brooks Koepka walked by. I looked at Carmen and mouthed, "Do you want him?"

Carmen shook his head vigorously, yes! I put my headset down and went running over to the door where Brooks was about to enter. I yelled, "Brooks." He turned around and I said, "Hey, do you have a few minutes to join us?" I was pointing to our set, ten steps from where he was standing. Brooks gave me an odd look and said, "No, man. I'm good" and walked into the clubhouse. I walked back and Carmen was laughing hysterically. He said on the air, "You are not going to believe what Merk just did. He approached, arguably the best golfer in the world, with chocolate ice cream all over his face. No wonder Brooks said no! I quickly looked in the mirror. I was a mess! To this day I still think Carmen set me up!

Rocco Mediate

You are probably thinking, how can you possibly have a story on Rocco Mediate? He is a PGA Golfer with not many wins to his name. Back in 2008, Rocco went on quite a run at the US Open at Torrey Pines. As a matter of fact, he had the lead in the clubhouse on Sunday and only two golfers on the course could catch him - Lee Westwood and Tiger Woods. Westwood missed a 20-footer downhill... and then there was one. Tiger Woods' putt rolled around the cup and went in. There would be a playoff between Tiger and Rocco.

Rocco is one of the most charismatic golfers on the tour. He is a great interview and always willing to talk. He was going to have an 18-hole playoff against Tiger on Monday, and they were going to tee off around 11 am central. I thought, "Boy, how amazing would it be to get Rocco on before he teed off against Tiger?" I started calling the hotels in San Diego until I found Rocco. I called his room and a gentleman answered. I said, "Rocco?" He responded, "No, but I'm standing right by him. What do you need?" I responded, "I'm calling with ESPN 1000. I wanted to see if he might have time tomorrow morning to join us before the round?" He said, "Interesting. Let me check." He returned a second later and said, "Rocco's in. How about around 8am pacific time?" I was actually kind of shocked but thrilled at the same time. He gave me his cell and asked me to text me fifteen minutes before as a reminder.

I remember the next morning vividly. Carmen was in for Silvy that day. He sat down next me and said, "Hey, Merk. What do we have today?" I said, "We are going to be golf intensive. We most likely will have Johnny Miller (future story) and I think we have Rocco Mediate at 10." Carmen looked at me and said, "Shut the f*** up! We aren't getting Rocco Mediate an hour before he tees off against Tiger!" I said, "Carm, I spoke to his rep last night and they said they would do it." He was shocked. I reached out to Rocco's guy at around 9:30 central. He responded right away and said, "Hey, I hate to do this, but Rocco was unaware of all his responsibilities before the round. I think he is going to have to pass, but I promise you we will join tomorrow win or lose at the same time." I said, "Done."

Well, Rocco lost in a great playoff against Tiger. It went 19 holes. The following day, as promised, he joined Waddle and Silvy and was fantastic. From the relationship that we built during the US Open, he came on a few other times, including right after Tiger's press conference when he was struggling with a sex addiction. I finally met Rocco in person in 2018 at the Senior Players Championship. He was very nice and remembered coming on with our station.

Greg Norman and Chris Evert

It was the 2008 Open Championship, and 53-year-old Greg Norman had the lead after three rounds. However, after the first round, Greg was only one shot off the lead. For a 53-year-old to be in contention at a major is a huge story. For the Shark to be in contention is even a bigger one. No one had more drama and more near misses in their career than Greg Norman. After round one, Greg was only a shot back. What a story!

I had never booked Greg Norman as a guest. It took me a while, but I found the hotel where he was staying. It was six hours ahead. At that time, Waddle and Silvy were on from 9am-12pm and I let them know I would be trying Greg. I called the hotel, and they rang his room. A woman answered on the first ring. I said, "Hi, is Greg there?"

"He is, but he just went down for a nap. Can I help you?"

I was thinking, didn't the Shark just marry Chris Evert? So I asked, "Is this Chris Evert?" She said it was. "It's Randy with ESPN 1000. Congratulations on a great first round!"

"Oh thank you. Isn't this so exciting?"

I said that it was great! She told me to feel free to try Greg back in a few hours. Maybe an hour after hanging up with her, I was kicking myself. I should have put Chris on talk about what the first day was like. That was my bad. I never did get Greg on and I only spoke to him once when I worked at One-On-One Sports. I still would love to book Greg Norman.

Justin Leonard

Justin Leonard is an accomplished golfer and one of my greatest bookings. It goes back to the '98 British Open. Justin was battling Darren Clarke and Jesper Parnevik to win the prestigious title. I happened to be watching the coverage on Saturday morning. When I watch golf coverage, I don't just watch for the golf. I look and listen for anything that could help my job.

On that day I saw the broadcasters show the clubhouse where the Open was being played. Then they said there was an attached hotel where a lot of the golfers were staying. I wrote the hotel down and when I got to work, I looked it up. I called during Sports Saturday and asked if Justin Leonard was staying there. They said he was and offered to ring the room. I declined but thanked the receptionist. Now I knew where he was staying. I figured that if he won the next day, I would be calling him.

Well, the next day Justin closed the deal and won the Open Championship. I was watching the post Championship coverage. He finished up his press conference and I waited half an hour and called Justin at the top of the hour. He answered right away. I congratulated him and asked if he would be willing to join us. He said, "Sure, do you need me to go downstairs?" I told him that we could do the interview over the phone. He said, "Sure, I will be happy to come on." He did ask, "Hey, how the heck did you find where I was staying?" I said, "It's my job!"

He was great. During his presser he broke down and started crying. I put him on with Bob Berger and Bruce Murray and they were able to ask him about it. I remember our update guy, Steve Olken, coming in the studio and asking where we got this cut from Justin. I said, "He's on the air live right now." He asked, "How the heck did you get him live? That's amazing." Anyways, it was one of the proudest moments I had as a guest booker.

Two years later, Justin was in contention again. I thought we had a pretty good relationship and I wanted to get him on before his final round. I called the hotel a few times, but it kept going to voicemail saying he was on the phone. Finally, at around 10:30am his time, he answered. He sounded wide awake. I asked if he could join us. He was not happy. He said I woke him up! I didn't see how that was possible, but I still apologized and wished him luck the next day. He said, "Wait a minute. I'm up now. Go ahead and do the interview." I sent Bruce Murray down to tape the interview. I put it in cue and as Bruce said, "Hey Justin, how are you doing?" He answered, "Your producer woke me up!" Well, he still did the interview. This is the life of a producer!

Scott Dunlap

Scott Dunlap is an accomplished PGA and now, Champions Tour, golfer. Back in August of 2000, Scott had a chance to win the PGA Championship. We were broadcasting for One-On-One

Sports live from the tournament in Louisville. Tiger Woods was in contention. Where our broadcast site was set up provided us a chance to bring almost every golfer over after their round, except for Tiger Woods. I would just wait for them after their press conference was done and bring them over. Most of them would be on with the late, great Chet Coppock. Chet had a flare for the dramatic and he often made an event or situation bigger than it was. However, Chet didn't know a lot about golf. So, before I brought over each golfer, I would give Chet a brief description about the golfer. I told Chet, "Hey, I'm about to bring over Scott Dunlap. He's a good golfer, but has never been able to win the big event. If he goes out tomorrow and beats Tiger, he is set for life!" Chet's eyes lit up.

I brought Scott over and told him he would be on with Chet Coppock. Chet started the interview and didn't even ask about his round. He said, "Let me lay it out for you Scott. You slay the Tiger tomorrow, and you are Madison Avenue's new favorite athlete. You can call your own shot. You win tomorrow and you have a minimum 5 million dollar pay day!" Scott looks at Chet like he's nuts. He said, "Well, I believe first place is just over a mil. I'm not quite sure where you are getting 5 mil from." Chet said, 'Trust me. You win you are set for life!" Scott kind of shrugged his shoulders and the interview lasted another minute before Chet let him go. After the golfers were done, I would walk them out. As I was walking Scott out, he turned me to and said, "Hey, the guy I was just talking to, Chuck? Is he all with it??"

"Yeah, why?"

"What the heck was he talking about?"

"Oh, that is Chet just trying to make you bigger than you are!" He laughed and I wished him well on Sunday. Unfortunately for Scott, Tiger was the winner that Sunday.

Johnny Miller

Johnny Miller is, in my opinion, the best golf analyst ever. However, at times, he can be very curt. Over the years, I have built a very good relationship with Johnny. He has joined Waddle and Silvy for some of the biggest moments in golf. Back in 2008, Tiger Woods was in battle with Rocco Mediate at the US Open at Torrey Pines. They were set for a playoff on Monday at 11am. I texted Johnny after the round was complete on Sunday. He didn't respond. I decided to call him an hour later. He always answers the same way. "Hello" kind of with a southern drawl.

"Johnny, it's Randy with ESPN 1000. How are you doing?"

He said he was fine.

"What a day!"

He was always a man of few words on the phone. He said, "It certainly was."

"Is there any chance you could join Waddle and Silvy tomorrow before the playoff?"

"Boy, Randy, that's going to be tough. I have to walk the course in the morning to see where all the pin placements are. I'll tell you what. Go ahead and call me if I have time, I will always do it."

Side note... I had also reached out to Rocco Mediate, but he cancelled that morning. So, I called Johnny at 10am that morning and Johnny answered.

"Hey Randy, I was waiting for your call. I have like five minutes right now. Does that work?"

"Let's do it!"

"I hope you don't mind, but I'm standing on the 18th green so you might hear some ambient sound."

I thought that was great.

Carmen was filling in for Silvy and the guys welcomed Johnny to the show. A couple of minutes into the interview they ask him about the putt Tiger hit on Sunday to send it into a playoff. He said, "Actually guys, right now I'm standing exactly where Tiger hit the putt. Let me tell you it was a lot tougher than it looked on TV."

I think the whole interview was eight minutes, but I couldn't get over how awesome he was with his time and how engaged he was with the interview. Johnny retired a few years ago and I reached out to him recently via text to see if he would join our golf podcast. He responded, "Randy, I am on vacation and retired, so I'll have to pass! Best wishes, Johnny." Love it! He always gets right to the point. I loved booking Johnny Miller.

Jack Nicklaus

Every weekend as a producer of the national radio show, *Sports Saturday and Sunday*, I always looked for that WOW guest. One weekend, I saw that the Senior Golf Tour was playing in Grand Blanc, Michigan on Friday, Saturday, and Sunday. Golf Legend Jack Nicklaus was in the field this week and it had been a goal of mine to book the *Golden Bear*. I found the hotel where the players were staying, which was the first hurdle. Jack Nicklaus had a 10:30 am tee time. I figured it would be a 4 ½ hour round, so I started calling him in the hotel around 3:30 pm. No one answered the first three times, but on the fourth try, Barbara Nicklaus answered. I said, "Hello Mrs. Nicklaus, it's Randy with One-On-One Sports. How are you?" She said, "Fine." I asked if Mr. Nicklaus was available. She responded, "Oh Randy, you just missed him. He went downstairs (in the hotel) to have dinner with some of the other players." I told her that I was trying to set up a phone interview with Mr. Nicklaus and she told me to try calling him after his round tomorrow. I thanked her very much for the help. FYI - It's always key to be extra polite to whoever answers the phone, especially if it's a spouse. Trust me, it helps!

That Saturday, I checked Jack's tee time, which was around 11:30 am. I was determined to get him on the air after his round. So, I started calling the hotel around 4pm. At 4:30, Barbara Nicklaus answered again. I said, "Hello Mrs. Nicklaus, it's Randy Merkin calling back from One-On-One Sports. Is there any chance Mr. Nicklaus is around?" She chuckled and said, "Oh Randy, you just missed him again! He's already downstairs. I'm meeting him for dinner soon." I was upset that my timing was off, but I asked if I could try to reach him the next day. She said, "Absolutely! I will let him know you are interested in having him on."

Sunday was the final round. My chief concern was that Jack wouldn't go back to the hotel after his round since he was headed across the pond to play in the Open. I checked his tee time, which was around 11am. I called the hotel at 3:30pm and, sure enough, Barbara Nicklaus answered. I said, "Hello Mrs. Nicklaus, it's Randy Merkin *again*, with One-On-One Sports. Is there any chance Mr. Nicklaus is around this time? She said, "Randy, you are not going to believe this, but he just went downstairs to check out and then we are headed to the airport to catch a flight to play in the Open." I couldn't contain my disappointment. "Boy, I guess I have rotten luck this week!" She offered, "I'll tell you what. Give me your number. If he has time, maybe he can call you on the ride to the airport." I gave her my number, but my feeling was that I missed out on my chance to book the *Golden Bear*.

I was still pondering the situation when I was about to leave the studio to take a break. As I was walking out, the producer I was working with said, "Merk, you have a call on hold." I walked into the studio and asked who was on the phone. He thought it was Joe Salvatore from San Francisco, who was a part of my stringer mob that covered games across the country. I answered the phone with a curt, "Yeah." I heard, "Randy, it's Jack Nicklaus. My wife said I should call this nice young man back. He's been very persistent." I was so glad that he called, but I realized how I had answered the phone, so I apologized to Mr. Nicklaus for not answering in a professional manner. He asked how he could help me, and I asked if he had five minutes to tape an interview with us right then. He answered, "Sure, we will be in the car for at least thirty minutes.

Take all the time you need." I sent our host, Scott Wetzel, down to the other studio. I sprinted down there myself to make sure it all went okay. Not only did it go well, it was fantastic - ten minutes of great radio!

The best part about that encounter is that I developed a good relationship with Mr. Nicklaus. Over the next four years, I had him on the radio at least four or five times. Each time, I was able to locate him in his hotel and each time he couldn't have been nicer. He is the best golfer of all time and a world class guy!

Two Holes in One

Sometimes you need to get away from the grind and remember that having fun matters. You can't be 24/7 all the time or you will burn out. One of my passions is golf. I love playing it, watching it, and betting on it. The crazy thing is that wasn't always the case. I can remember watching Jack Nicklaus winning in 1986, but I didn't watch golf religiously until I started working with Bob and Bruce at One-On-One Sports. They loved golf and it made me have a passion for the sport.

It's every golfer's dream to have a hole in one. You hear stories from golfers who say that they came so close to a hole in one. Well, until 2004, I could only think of a few instances when I came close to a hole in one. Until this... It was a warm day towards the end of May, and I was playing golf with Chet Coppock. Because of our schedules, Chet and I had Monday and Tuesday off. If the weather was nice, we played golf at least one of those days. This particular day we were at Deerfield Golf Course in Riverwoods, IL. At the time, it was the 7th hole and probably 135 yards. The flag was tucked behind the trap. Chet went first and pushed his shot to the right. I was next up. I grabbed a 7 iron and hit it pure. I knew instantly that it was a good shot. I saw it land on the front of the green and head towards the hole, but I couldn't see the hole from the tee box. I heard a loud click. I yelled to Chet, "I think that went in!" He responded, "Ah Merk, you are crazy. That's over the green." I jumped as high as I could, but I couldn't see the ball. I screamed, "I got a hole in one!" I jumped into Chet's arms. He was shocked! There were four older gentlemen playing on the next hole and I yelled to them, "I just got a hole in one!" They didn't seem to care. We drove up to the hole and I jumped out of the cart and went running to the hole. The ball was right in the cup! I went nuts again! I placed the ball in the cart in the little compartment in front of me. When we were on the back 9, all of sudden, I noticed the ball was gone! I said, "Chet, where is the ball?" He looked at me and said, "Merk, you will always have the memories." I said, "Turn the cart around!" We went back to the previous tee box and there it was! After the round, it is customary to buy drinks for anyone in the clubhouse. Well, I went into the clubhouse and there were the same four old guys. I said, "Drinks are on me. I just got my first hole in one!" They just all looked at me and kept playing cards. I said, "Oh well," and left. Everyone told me that I will never get another hole in one because I didn't buy drinks.

Two days later I was playing golf after work at Sportsman's Country Club in Northbrook, IL with my good friend, Rob Wuzyzinski. We were joined by a nice man, who did not speak English, while playing on the 9-hole course. Man, it was a slow round. I was supposed to bring home dinner after golf, and I told Beth it would be around 6. It was 5:45 and we were only through 7 holes. I called Beth and asked what she wanted me to do. She said that she was hungry, and that I should finish up. I agreed and I told Rob that I was going to leave. He said, "Well, 8 is on your way in. You might as well play 8." I thought that was a good call. The 8th hole was a 125 par 3 and the flag was in the middle of the green. I pulled out a 7 iron and hit it pure. I knew it was a good shot. It's like I read the green from the tee box and knew exactly where it was going. It landed on the front of the green and literally just tracked right towards the hole. Its last spin was in the hole. I threw my club in the air and screamed, "I did it again!" I started sprinting towards the hole. As I was sprinting, Rob was teeing up golf balls trying to hit me and the nice man we played with was signaling touchdown and screaming!

I grabbed the ball out of the hole and put it in my pocket. Of course, I had to play the 9th hole. Little did I know, if I didn't play the 9th hole, it wouldn't have counted officially as a hole in one. After the round, I went into the clubhouse at Sportsman's. I told the folks there that I just had my second hole in one in 3 days and that drinks were on me! Several people took me up on the drink. One gentleman came up to me and asked, "What did you use"? When I told him that I used a 7 iron for 125 yards, he said, "I wouldn't let anyone know that!"

A year later, I was at Sportsman's again playing the 3rd hole and it was 155 uphill. I hit a great 5 iron. I was playing with an older couple. The ball landed right next to the hole and took one little hop behind the hole and stopped. It looked like it went it. The old couple yelled from their tee box that it went it in. I knew better, but I came that close to number 3! Years later, my lovely wife made an awesome shadow box for me with the scorecards, the balls, and the certificates from each hole in one. It's something I cherish. To this day, it is my greatest sports achievement.

BOXING, HOCKEY, HORSES & TENNIS

John McEnroe

It was 1999 and I had been producing *Sports Saturday and Sunday with Bob Berger and Bruce Murray* for about five years. During that time, I had never booked Tennis Great John McEnroe. I loved watching "Johnny Mac" while growing up. By the time I got into the profession, Mac was retired so there weren't many opportunities to book him because he was no longer playing. The main reason I wanted him on the show is because, in my opinion, he is one of most entertaining, thoughtful interviews in sports.

In the summer of 1999, I finally had my chance to book John McEnroe. He was going into the Tennis Hall of Fame. I knew he would be staying at a hotel in Newport, Rhode Island, but the problem was finding out which one. I looked up nice hotels in Newport and one was The Viking. I called to see if he was registered. He was! I told the operator that I would call back and, in the meantime, I prepared Bob Berger and Bruce Murray to tape the interview with him.

The ceremony was on Saturday morning, so I figured he would probably be in his room on Friday afternoon. I called the hotel and asked for John McEnroe's room. On the third ring, someone answered the phone and it turned out to be his daughter. As a guest booker, that's usually not good because there is not a high success rate when the family is in the room. She asked who was calling I said it was Randy from One-On-One Sports in Chicago. She called out, "Dad, it's some guy from a radio station in Chicago." He picked up the phone and muttered, "Hello." I said, "Hey John, it's Randy with One-On- One Sports. Congratulations!"

"Thanks. What do you want?"

"Is there a chance you have a few minutes to tape an interview with my hosts, Bob Berger and Bruce Murray, about going into the Hall of Fame?"

He did not seem happy and responded with, "Let's see here...

you want me to do a radio interview right now with my four kids, my wife Patti, Patrick and his family and my parents all with me? You cannot be serious!" I told John that it would last just ten minutes tops. He responded, "Absolutely not and don't call back!" and hung up. Bruce Murray was listening and said, "Well, I'm guessing that was a no?" I figured my best shot to get McEnroe on the air was over and I was super disappointed.

The following day, I was producing *Sports Saturday* and I looked up at the TV around 2pm. I saw a replay of John's speech from the Hall of Fame, and I contemplated calling him again. I thought, what's the worst he can do - hang up on me again? I told Bob and Bruce about my plan to try again, and they encouraged me to give it another try. When I called the hotel and asked for John's room, his daughter answered again. I asked, "Hi, is your dad around?" She shouted, "Dad, it's the sports radio guy who called yesterday." He quickly picked up the phone and said, "You again! Didn't you get the point yesterday?" I calmly said, "Hey, John! Congrats! It looked like a great ceremony." He told me that he was not doing the interview, and, in that moment, I decided to use another strategy. I said, "John, you must need a break from your family!" He paused for about three seconds and then showed a change in his demeanor. "You know what? That's a great call!" He then yelled out to his family, "Listen up! I'm about to do a radio interview. I'm going into the other room and can't be bothered for twenty minutes." I told John that all we needed was ten minutes, but he quickly responded, "You'll do twenty!"

I sent Bob and Bruce down to the other studio and they taped a great wide-ranging interview with John McEnroe. I was very pleased with the result. I use this story as a reminder that sometimes the producer has to do some dirty work to get the end result.

Wayne Gretzky

There are times in this job when I have to pinch myself since I get to deal with a lot of amazing people, including elite athletes. One of the top athletes, without a doubt, is the Great One, Wayne Gretzky. Back in the day, like the early 2000's, everyone was having celebrity golf tournaments. Most players usually teed off around 1 or 2pm and were back in their hotel rooms by 6pm. I was working weekends back then producing Bob & Bruce. Sometimes I had to stay until 10pm as well to produce Larry Cotlar.

Mario Lemieux always had his golf tourney in late June, and I would print out his celebrity guest list. It was the "who's who" in most major sports that weren't playing at the time. I had my eye on one guy - Wayne Gretzky. I have never booked him, but I found the hotel and called Wayne around 7pm. He answered right away, and he couldn't have been nicer. I asked if he might be willing to join Larry. He said he would. Usually stars like Wayne only do interviews for people they know, but not Wayne. He came on with Larry and gave him ten minutes. I booked him at the same tourney the following year, but this time on a Sunday night. When we wrapped up, he told the host to say "hi" to Chet Coppock, because the first hockey team where Wayne played was in Indy, where Chet also got his start.

When I moved to ESPN 1000, I felt like it was a clean slate. I wanted to get Wayne on ESPN as well, and I had the perfect opportunity when the Cubs drafted his son, Trevor. I reached out to his PR company and they helped set it up. He was great! He gave Waddle and Silvy about fifteen minutes of his time. Over the next several years, Wayne Gretzky was on ESPN 1000 numerous times. As a matter of fact, one time JD was in for Waddle, and I got Wayne to call in to wish JD a happy birthday. The hook was that it was also Wayne's birthday. He's that nice of a guy. Another time, he came on right after we had Peyton Manning on! What a dynamic duo. When Stan Mikita passed away, I texted Wayne and asked if he could come on to talk about Stan since I know Wayne thought very highly of Stan. Of course, he came on. Am I making my point? Wayne Gretzky might be a top five player of our generation, but he was always willing to join us.

One story that always will be special to me was the year when the Hawks were battling the Redwings in the Western Conference Semi-Finals. Wayne had joined us already once during the play-offs, which was the day after the Hawks fell behind the wings 3-1. I remember his optimistic take on the air. He thought that the Hawks were still going to win the series and they were going to win the Cup. I remember when he was done with Waddle and Silvy, I picked up the line to thank him. He said, "Randy, don't worry about this series. The Hawks are going to win!"

Back then, I had a Blackberry and it wasn't working too well. I took it to the Verizon store and they told me I needed a new battery. So, I could either pay for a battery at that time or they could order one for me free of charge. The only problem is it would take three business days. You have to understand that my phone was key to me doing my job well. I thought it would be cool to see how I could do my job without my Blackberry. In a given day, I can receive up to 100 texts. I remember saying to my wife Beth, "I wonder what the coolest text will be I will receive during the three-day span."

I got the FedEx slip that my battery was in and I went to the store in Northbrook to pick it up. I put in the battery and the texts started to load! There were a lot of texts, but one stood out! Wayne Gretzky texted me unsolicited. The Hawks had just taken out the Wings the night before and the text read, "I told you, Randy, the Hawks had it all the way. I hope you are well. Let me know if you need me in the next round." I was shocked and couldn't believe that Wayne Gretzky took the time to text me. This is something I will always remember.

Floyd Mayweather

Pound for pound, he's probably the greatest fighter of our lifetime. Floyd Mayweather doesn't do many interviews. He doesn't need to. However, I was able to get him twice. The first time was back in 2011 when Floyd posted a winning ticket on betting on the Bulls and Derrick Rose in the first half of a game. He claimed he won over $37,000.00. That intrigued me because of the Bulls tie-in, so I reached out to my friend Bernie Barhamsel, who is very big in the boxing community. I asked him if he had a phone number for Floyd. He gave me a contact for Floyd's uncle, so I reached out to him. It took many texts and calls, but finally I convinced him to have Floyd call into *The Waddle and Silvy Show*. He called a little late, but was great with the guys. He talked about some of his big winnings and big losses.

The second booking with Floyd was actually in studio. Floyd had a big fight coming up and was doing a press conference across the street at the Chicago Theater. Thanks to my good friends, Roman Modrowski and Ray Flores, I was able to get a contact for Floyd. His PR person was helpful and through multiple emails, I was able to convince her to have Floyd come to our studio before he went across the street for his presser.

We arranged for Floyd to come through the back door. We had promoted his appearance for a day or two and there must have been 150 to 200 people in front of our State Street studio to get a glimpse of Floyd! Some were waiting for autographs. Our Marketing Director had ten boxing gloves for Floyd to sign. When he walked in, he was ready to sign, but his PR department nixed that right away. They said he was only there for an interview. I also had purchased a glove for him to sign for my son, Brett. When he went into the studio, I brought the glove and asked if he would sign it for my son. He said, "Absolutely!" (The glove is still in our basement with some of the other great memorabilia I got for Brett.)

Floyd was joined by quite the entourage. He had two gigantic bodyguards. Floyd sat down in the studio and was very friendly with Waddle and Silvy. I asked Floyd, like I ask most guests, if I could get him something to drink. He asked me, "Are you being real?"

"I am."

"Let's see if you can pull this off. I want a big glass of lukewarm water. Not too hot or cold. Lukewarm. Can you handle it?"

"You got it" I assured him.

I went into the ABC Green Room and took a big glass and filled it up with half cold and half hot water. I let it sit for five minutes and brought it to Floyd when he was on the air. When we went to break, I went in the studio to talk to the guys. Floyd said, "Hey man, nice job with the water. It hit the spot!"

It was one of the crazier scenes I have witnessed from our State Street studio. I couldn't believe how big the crowd was outside! Floyd walked out after the interview and there were many people waiting to meet him. He was very gracious with his time. This, of course, is the tough part of my job... I know Floyd has a checkered past and allegedly has done some things that are downright despicable. In this industry, however, you have to realize you aren't going to be dealing with choir boys or girls, and fans still want to hear from their favorite athletes.

Mike Eruzione and Al Michaels

February 22, 1980 is a memorable day for most USA Hockey fans. It is, of course, the day the USA pulled the greatest upset of all time and beat the unbeatable Russians! On another note, it's a big deal for me because my life changed forever on February 22, 2007, when my twins were born.

I think every sports radio producer has Mike Eruzione's cell phone. He currently works for the University of Boston as a consultant. Usually, a few days before the anniversary of the game, Mike gets bombarded with calls. He probably does 20-30 interviews on that day and he probably lives for this day every year. I am one of those producers who calls Mike every year. When I asked Waddle and Silvy if they wanted to talk with Mike, they said "Sure, he's a great interview" and Waddle always liked talking to Boston guys.

It's always been my philosophy to make the interview stand out. I knew on this day that most shows would talk with either Mike Eruzione, Jack O'Callahan or Jim Craig. At this point, I had a decent relationship with Al Michaels. I have called him in a hotel a few times before a big game. He was always gracious with his time. Al was in Vancouver Canada with NBC for the Winter Olympics. If you don't remember, Al Michaels was the voice who called that historic game, *you believe in miracles, Yes!* I figured, why not call Al and surprise Mike Eruzione? The only problem was finding Al in Vancouver. It took some digging, but I found him. I called the hotel before Mike was coming on to try and set up Al, but he was on the phone. I put Mike on with Waddle and Silvy and let them know there was an outside chance that Al might join us. I called Al back, knowing this was my final shot. He answered! I explained the situation.

"Randy, tell Mike I say hello, but I am way late."

"Al, I was just looking for three minutes."

He paused for a second and said, "Go ahead."

Waddle and Silvy welcomed Al in. Mike was thrilled. They were on the air for close to ten minutes. Memorable stories were shared by both guys and I'm glad I went that extra mile to make a good interview great.

The Kentucky Derby

We did our show for three or four straight years from the Kentucky Derby. We did the show from 12-6pm and then hightailed it out of there to make the 6:50pm Southwest flight to Chicago. I always felt like we weren't able to do our shows how we wanted to because we were concerned about making that flight. Finally, we decided to drive to Louisville. Yes, it was a long drive, but at least we didn't have to rush out of there after the broadcast.

So I thought we were all set for a great broadcast. We had taped a bunch of good interviews. The only problem that day was the weather. It was terrible. For some reason, it was impacting our connection with the station and our line must have dropped several times in the first hour. It was a nightmare broadcast. Some on our interviews didn't run correctly and our line kept dropping. Plus, our engineer decided to leave the broadcast and go to the grandstand to watch the race! Let's just say we were excited to get out of there.

It was a very quiet ride home with Bob and Bruce. Not much was being said. We all wanted to do a great show and it just didn't happen. I was driving, thinking, "Man, this is going to be a long six hours." We were probably a half hour in when a car pulled up alongside us with six college-age girls. It looked like they had come from the Derby. They honked and told me to roll down my window. They asked, "Hey, did you guys come from the Derby?" I said that we did. They asked, "Did you have fun?"

"Not really. We were broadcasting and our line dropped a bunch of times." As I was saying this, I was thinking that they don't care! They all said, "Oh, were sorry to hear that. Here's something to cheer you up." It all happened so quickly - all five girls were leaning out of the windows and they all took their tops off! We didn't know what to do. We just gave them a thumbs up. They sped up and we didn't see them again. However, it made a terrible day tolerable for at least a minute!

Mike Tyson

When I was growing up, any Mike Tyson fight was must-see TV. You would plan your whole night around it. I remember where I was in college when he lost to Buster Douglas. I remember having a roundtable discussion with my fraternity brothers afterwards to discuss that historic loss. Had I known that fifteen years later I would be booking Mike Tyson as a guest, I'd have been shocked. I remember the first time I booked the Champ for Waddle and Silvy. I was in Las Vegas on vacation with my lovely wife, Beth. While most people listen to music by the pool, I was listening to Las Vegas sports radio. I heard they were going to have Mike Tyson on, and I was curious how he was as a guest. He was good! During the interview, they promoted that the following weekend he was going to be in Chicago at an autograph show. A bell went off in my head. Even though I was on vacation, I was going to book Mike Tyson.

I first called the producer for Waddle and Silvy and asked if they wanted to speak with the Champ. Of course they did! My next step was to call ESPN Las Vegas and speak to the host. I believe his name was Cete Williams. I left a message and he called me right back. I was very complimentary of his show because I really did like it. I then said that we wanted Mike on as a guest and, believe it or not, he said that Mike was his good friend. He said the best way to book Mike was to go through his wife, Kiki. He gave me her cell and I contacted her. She called me back right away and said she would check with Mike.

I vividly remember when she called back. We were headed into a show at the Venetian when I saw her number pop up, so I jumped out of line to find a quiet place. She said Mike would be happy to come on. She took down all the info and we were all set. The next day at 1pm Vegas time, Mike Tyson was on the air with Waddle & Silvy. He was good! I was pretty proud of myself since I made this happen while on vacation. I started to think, "Man, how great would it be to get Mike in studio!"

A few years later, that's what happened! I saw that Mike was in town again for another collectible show. I reached out to Kiki and she put me in touch with Mike's marketing team. They were outstanding. He was already scheduled to be on *Windy City Live*, which was the local talk show on ABC 7. Their studios were literally right down the hall from us, so it worked out perfectly. He was going on with them at 11am, so he would come in studio around 10am with Waddle and Silvy. I have to admit that I was a little nervous. I greeted Mike in the lobby with his PR team and he was very nice. We were walking back to our State Street studio when I turned to him and said, "Hey Champ, this means a lot that you are doing this." He put his arm around me and said, "You got it, Buddy. I'm just happy you want me on."

I introduced him to the guys. He was very friendly and the interview was a huge hit. On the screen I had a show rundown typed up. I told Silvy in his ear, "Tell Mike to preview the rest of the show." He did it, no problem. It was pure gold and we continued to use it for years to come. After he was done, there were about fifteen people outside of the studio looking for pictures and autographs. He was more than accommodating.

A couple of years later, Mike came back in studio with Carmen and Jurko to promote his one-man show. I was always kicking myself that I didn't have him sign a boxing glove for my son, but here was another opportunity. He happily signed one for my son and Danny Zederman's son. Not only that, but he remembered me from the last time he was in studio. This is one of my great memories in this industry - booking and meeting Mike Tyson!

Side note - I actually met Mike Tyson in 2005 at the Mandalay Bay workout room. I got there at 8am and was stretching when I saw Mike come in – with no entourage. He was just by himself. It was literally the two of us. He walked by me and said, "Hey, what's up, Buddy?" I was so nervous that I responded, "Hey Champ, looking good." Then he jumped on a treadmill and got to work.

Evander Holyfield

You won't meet a nicer guy than Evander Holyfield. Over the years I booked him to promote numerous fights. Whether it was through a PR firm or calling him in a hotel, he was always a willing participant. However, the story I am telling here has nothing to do with Evander being on the air.

Each day I try to look at who is having a birthday. I saw that it was Evander's birthday and I sent him a text wishing him a good day. Later that day, he responded and said, "Thank you, Randy." I figured that was the end of our exchange. The next day at 6am I received a text from Evander with a bible verse. I thought, "Oh, that's a nice gesture." The following day, and the following 2 weeks at exactly the same time, I received a bible verse from Evander and words of encouragement. I didn't really know how to respond, so about every third text I would simply say, "Thank you." He would respond, "You are welcome." This went on for probably 3 weeks before he stopped sending messages.

Reflecting back on it, I thought how cool it was for the former champ to take time out of his day to brighten mine!

MEDIA

Jim Nantz

Jim Nantz is probably the lead voice of our generation. Not only is he the lead voice, but he is one super nice human being. I had booked Jim a few times over the phone, but had never met him in person. I saw that he was going to be signing the book that he wrote on his late father at Borders on State Street. This was right down the street from our studios, so I reached out to his assistant, Melissa, who is the best. I asked her if Jim would have time to swing by before his book signing at noon. She let me know that his schedule was very tight that day, but he would try and make it work.

About a week later, she reached out and said Jim could stop by around 11am, but he would absolutely have to be gone by 11:30. I assured her that was not a problem, so we worked out all the logistics and everything was set. I met Jim down in the lobby around 10:55. He couldn't have been a nicer guy. On the way up on the elevator, I told him he was going to be on with Waddle and Silvy. He responded quickly, "You mean Tom Waddle, the Academic All-American from BC and their all-time leading receiver? You mean the guy on the Bears that was always willing to go over the middle and make the big catch? And, of course, Silvy has become one of the most respected talk show hosts in Chicago." I simply responded, "Wow, you made my job easy!" I thanked him for coming and he said, "Thank you, Randy, for giving me the opportunity."

I brought him in the studio with Waddle and Silvy and there was instant chemistry. I reminded Silvy that Jim had to be gone by 11:30, but he informed the guys he wanted to stay later, and he was good for another fifteen minutes. It was great radio! Of course, we all know Jim's voice, right? He's the voice of the Masters. I had five liners that I typed out for him to read after he was done, but I realized that probably wasn't going to happen. He finished the interview and gathered his stuff up quickly to make his noon book signing. As he was walking out, I thanked him and said, "Jim, any chance you have two minutes to record these liners?" Without thinking twice, he said, "Of course, Randy."

Billy Zuirekat and I went into Studio B to record the liners. Like the pro that he is, Jim did everything in one take. I told him, "This is awesome. We can't thank you enough, Jim." He paused for a second and said, "You know what Randy? I wasn't really happy with a couple of my reads. Can we do another take?" I quickly responded, "They were outstanding, but that's fine, Jim." He did them again and then asked Billy to play them back to make sure they were good. I was amazed, thanked him again, and walked him out. Oh, and it was now 11:55 and he barely made it in time for his book signing. A week later, we received a hand-written note from Jim thanking us for having him on. I wasn't surprised. Jim Nantz is pure class!

Dick Enberg

Who is one of the top three voices of sports broadcasting over the last fifty years? That is Dick Enberg. It was tourney time and Dick Enberg was doing four games on Friday with Jay Bilas. Waddle and Silvy were on remote that day. I called Dick in the hotel and asked him if he could join the guys in 20 minutes. He said, "Sure." I let the guys know down the line. He came on and previewed his four games for Friday and it was great having the legend on our show. At the end of the interview, he said he would be in town a month from then promoting his one-man show on Al McGuire. He said he would love to come on and talk about it. Of course, we wanted him, so when I picked up the phone after the interview, he gave me his email address.

I waited a couple of weeks and sent him an email to secure a time for the interview about the one-man show. However, I suggested he come in studio. It's better to have your guest in studio if it's possible because you always get more out of them. He agreed to come in and we set it up for Tuesday at 11am. Tuesdays at 10:30 on *The Waddle and Silvy Show* we did a segment called *Would you*

Rather? It was fun segment, but at times could be a little over-the-top. We would get calls with people asking questions like "Would you rather spend an hour with Charlie Weis or Jurko after they ate a bowl of baked beans?"

So, I'm getting ready to line up calls for WYR, when I get a call from the front desk at 10:28 saying that Dick Enberg is in the lobby. My heart sank. What should I do? I couldn't bring him during *Would You Rather*? Silvy already told me he didn't want to move the segment. My plan was to go down at 10:44 during the break and bring him up and put him in the conference room. I had the idea to turn down the volume of the programming in the office. At 10:32, Ernie Scatton, our production director, came in the studio and said, "Hey Merk, I saw Dick Enberg downstairs, so I brought him up. He is in the conference room." I remember thinking, "This isn't going to end well."

I walked over to the conference room and, before I could say anything, Dick held up his hand and said, "I know I'm early. I will just sit here in the conference room and read the paper." I thanked him for understanding, but there was one problem. I forgot to turn down the volume of the programming! I was horrified since WYR was really obnoxious on that day.

I went back to get him around 10:55 and, thank goodness, he didn't seem any worse for wear. I brought him in studio and introduced him to Waddle and Silvy. For the next 40 minutes, he was absolutely amazing. He told story after story about his Hall-of-Fame career. The best part of the interview was when he said, "You know, when I was sitting in your conference room waiting to come on, I was looking at the picture of Walter Payton. It brought back so many great memories." He then proceeded to tell two great stories about Walter that we had never heard. It was one of the best interviews Waddle and Silvy ever conducted. Dick Enberg's signature call was "Oh my" and his email was even DeOHMY@aol.com. Classic stuff. We miss Dick Enberg!

Tom Brokaw

The 1996 Summer Olympics were a big deal for One-On-One Sports. We sent a huge crew to Atlanta where we were going to be broadcasting many of the events on the in-house feed. With almost everyone in Atlanta, we had a very small staff in Northbrook, including myself.

It was around 4:30am on Saturday and I received a call from my boss, Mark Gentzkow, from Atlanta telling me that a bomb went off overnight and that I needed to wake up Bob and Bruce and get them on the air no later than 9am. I was pretty confused because they normally started at noon. I asked how long he wanted them to stay on the air. Mark just said, "Until I tell you guys to stop. They are going to be on for a long time." I woke up both Bob and Bruce and let them know that we would be starting around 9am.

When we got to the station, we met for a few minutes to discuss our plan. Obviously, this was a huge story, and it would be the focus of most of our show. I was going to try and get as much reaction from Atlanta as I could. Throughout our show, I noticed that Tom Brokaw was on the air for a very long time anchoring NBC's coverage. I thought he would be great to get on after he was done, so I started calling the Atlanta hotels to find where NBC was staying. After trying several hotels, I finally found where the NBC staff was staying. I was monitoring the TVs and watching for when Tom finished broadcasting. Finally, after about six hours on the air, Tom was done. I let Bob and Bruce know that I was going to try Tom Brokaw at the top of the hour and they both wished me good luck.

I called the hotel and asked for Tom Brokaw's room. After five rings, a sleepy Tom Brokaw answered the phone. In his famous gravelly voice, he answered the phone. I said, "Mr. Brokaw, it's Randy with One-On-One Sports. You have been doing an amazing job on the air." He asked how he could help me. I said, "Is there any chance you might have three minutes to join One-On-One Sports to update what's going on?" He seemed annoyed when he responded, "You have the nerve to wake me up and ask me to come on after I've been on the air for the last six hours?" I told him it would only be for like three minutes. He paused and said, "Go ahead and put me on." I quickly typed up on the screen to go to Tom Brokaw *now*! Bob and Bruce, as usual, did an amazing job transitioning and brought Tom on the show. The coolest part was that Tom had been sound asleep five minutes earlier, but once he was on the air, he sounded wide awake. After the interview, I picked up the phone to thank him. He grunted, "I'm going back to sleep."

Obviously, I had hoped to book Mr. Brokaw under better circumstances. However, it was still very cool to have one of the great voices of our generation on with Bob and Bruce.

Al Michaels

Al Michaels is one of my favorites. I'm not sure how far back our relationship goes, but it I feel privileged to sort of consider Al a friend. I used to book Al before each Thursday night season opener. I would call him in the hotel the day of the game and he would always do the interview. After a while, he recognized who I was. Later, I started emailing Al to come on whether he was doing a big Bears game or the Monday after the Super Bowl. He always came on. Over the years, he developed a great relationship with Waddle and Silvy. As a guest booker, that is remarkable. I've been really lucky in my career because I have worked with some great hosts who get it. First, it was Bob Berger and Bruce Murray, then Bob Stelton in for Bruce, and then Waddle and Silvy. Waddle and Silvy are so good at their job that it made it easy after a while to book big names. Al Michaels was one of the guests. After a few times as a guest, he came on and said, "This is my favorite show to come on." Sometimes you are thinking he is saying that about every show, but with Al, I believe it.

Here are two of the most memorable interviews with Al. The first was the day after the Patriots came back against the Falcons. Having Al on the day after the greatest comeback in Super Bowl History was special. The other happened December 2019. Al was at the reunion for the 1980 USA Hockey team. He spent twenty minutes with Waddle and Silvy going in depth about how much that game meant to him, how he got to call that game and what he loves about Vegas. Why did I like it so much? It made Al sound just like a regular guy!

Two years ago, Al came to town to broadcast the Bears vs Vikings game and then, two weeks later, the Bears vs Rams. These games were both late adds. I told Waddle and Silvy that instead of asking Al to come on, we should set him up at Chicago Cut restaurant as a thank you. I reached out to Al and asked if that would work for him. He told me that it would be great. We went back and forth and finally settled on a time. I emailed Al the morning of his reservation and told him to let me know if he needed anything. Later that night, around 11:30pm, I received an email from Al saying "Wow - what a place! Grand Slam home run, Randy! We already have our reservation for the Rams game." So, not only did I help develop the relationship with Al and Waddle and Silvy, but also with Al and Chicago Cut. Thanks, as always, to David Flom for his hospitality.

The following year, the Bears opened the season against the Packers at home on a Thursday night. The night before, the whole Sunday night crew had their dinner at Chicago Cut. Sometimes I have to take a step and back and think about how fortunate I am to work with such great people.

Big Cat

Big Cat is one of the greatest success stories in sports media over the past ten years. I remember him as Dan Katz. It was back in 2015 and David Kaplan had just been hired by ESPN 1000 to host 12-2pm. I was Kap's producer, and we were trying out different co-hosts with Kap. One day, our program director Adam Delevitt, came into my office and said "Hey, for the next two days, we are going to have Dan Katz, better known as Barstool Big Cat, host with Kap." I was like, "Who?" He said that he is a talented young guy. I talked to Dan the day before to go over some particulars.

He came into my office pretty early the day of his first show and told me a little about himself. He said that he was really tight with some of the Hawks and with Anthony Rizzo. I was really impressed with his connections, his hustle and what a good guy he was. He did two shows with Kap and he was great - very comfortable right away. Those were the only shows he did with Kap, but he came on the station from time to time.

Within the next couple of years, Barstool Big Cat and the whole Barstool brand had blown up! In 2018 Adam Delevitt said that we just made a huge hire. We got Big Cat for a weekly with Waddle and Silvy. No one had a bigger following with the younger crowd. My son's travel baseball coach, Landon Cohen, said to me after a game, "Great hire with Big Cat. He's the best and is an amazing follow on Twitter." Well, Barstool has even gotten bigger since then. However, one thing has never changed. He is as down to earth and as great a guy as he was when I worked with him in 2015. I'm not kidding when I say that some of my friends are more impressed that I am friends with Big Cat than with Charles Barkley or Al Michaels!

CELEBRITIES

Eddie Vedder

Eddie Vedder is a top 5 rock and roll musician of all time and a huge Cubs fan. Never did I think I would have the opportunity to book Eddie. It all started before a Cubs playoff game against the Mets in the 2015 NLCS. David Kaplan was on the field before the game talking to some players when Eddie Vedder approached him. He told Kap that he is a huge fan of him and Todd Hollandsworth. Kap told Eddie to come on his radio show. Eddie was excited, so Kap got his cell phone and gave it to me the next morning. I texted Eddie and he didn't respond right away. (He never does!) A couple of days later he responded, and we set up a time. He was outstanding! During his interview, he mentioned how he recruited Theo to the Cubs, and he dropped like 3 f-bombs! We dumped them all. After his interview with Kap, he texted me apologizing for swearing. He said he got caught up in the moment.

It's weird but through our brief text exchanges, I felt like we actually had a slight connection. Later that year, the guys at the station were having issues getting tickets to Eddie's concerts at Wrigley. I told Danny Zederman that we have the best connection - Eddie Vedder himself! I texted Eddie asking if it was possible to get tickets for the guys. A week later, he texted back that we were all set and to just contact him as the concert dates got closer. Of course, he came through in a big way. Our connection continued. He didn't always respond to my text, but when he did, it was worth the wait. I tried to book him after the Cubs win in 2016. He responded a few days later saying he was at a benefit concert, but added, "I still can't believe we made it to the summit! The view up here is INCREDIBLE!"

We exchanged a few texts for Cubs opening day in 2017. The next text exchange was classic. Danny Zederman is the biggest Pearl Jam fan I know. I asked Eddie if there was any way he could call in for Danny's birthday. I didn't receive any response during the show when Danny was producing. However, later that day, I saw a video pop up on my phone with Eddie's face on it. He had recorded himself singing "Happy Birthday" to Danny. I was shocked and it was amazing! Danny, of course, went nuts. The video went viral! That summer, again, he helped all of us with tickets for his shows at Wrigley. I went with my wife, Beth. NO question, it was the best concert I ever attended. Simply amazing.

The coolest thing about this text friendship is that Eddie never met me, and our only connection was the Cubs. He's an amazing human! My kids B'nai Mitzvah was a couple of months away and we were compiling famous people to record messages for them. I had Bar Stool Big Cat, Kyle Long, Jeff Garlin and Charles Barkley. I thought it would be amazing to finish with Eddie Vedder. I sent him the text and he responded that he would be happy to do it and to just remind him. I sent him a couple of reminders and he finally came through with an amazing video. It is probably in the top three moments as a guest booker. For Eddie to take the time to record such a great video was very gracious. He was the anchor in my kids' B'nai Mitzvah video.

I don't always text Eddie with requests. I often text him after a Cubs win or when he has a great performance. Sometimes he responds and sometimes he doesn't. I hope he understands how much I treasure the videos he has sent and the fact that he takes the time to acknowledge my texts. These are life-changing moments for me. Thanks Eddie!!

Donny Osmond

The great Donny Osmond is a legendary star of stage and screen. You might be wondering how my path crossed with Donny Osmond? Well, it's very simple. Donny and his sister Marie were in Chicago doing a show. They were staying at a hotel not far from our State Street studio and every morning on his way to rehearse for his show, Donny would walk by our studio and stop to say "hi" to Waddle and Silvy. He would always mouth to Waddle, "How did the Giants do, or how did the 9ers do?" He was a big fan of the San Francisco teams.

In the studio where I was set up, I couldn't always see who was walking by outside. Every time Donny would walk by Waddle would say, "My buddy Donny Osmond just walked by." I would say, "Did you ask him to come in studio?" He said, "No, I didn't want to bother him." I told him to give me a heads up the next time Donny walked up, and I would go grab him.

So a few weeks went by and Donny came by the studio again. This time, Mark Giangreco was in studio as well. On the air, Waddle was trying to carry on a conversation with Donny through the glass. Great radio! As Donny was leaving, I asked Waddle on air, "Did you ask him to come in studio??" Again, Waddle responded, "no." I yelled on the air, "Come on, Waddle!" I dropped my headphones and, in a mad sprint, ran out of the studio to talk to Donny. *Windy City Live* was about to begin taping and I had to weave my way through the audience. I ran all the way down State Street to Randolph. Donny was about to cross the street when I screamed, "Donny wait!" He turned around and I said, "I'm Randy with ESPN. You have to come back and go on the air with Waddle and Silvy." He said, "All right. I'll do it!" I walked him through the Windy City Live audience. They were all yelling, "There's Donny Osmond!" I walked him in the studio, and he joked that Waddle and Silvy didn't give him a good enough ovation, like the other audience. It was a great interview! Donny and Giangreco actually lived right by each other when Donny was here doing *Joseph and the Amazing Technicolor Dreamcoat*. I was very happy that we were finally able to get Donny on the air and that he was such a good guest.

Jack Lemmon

The Pebble Beach Pro Am is always a highlight of the year for a sports show producer. Not only do you have a great field of golfers, but there are always top-notch celebrities as well. One of the main stories each year was Jack Lemmon's quest to make the cut since he had achieved this goal. My hosts, Bob Berger and Bruce Murray, loved Jack Lemmon. Every year they asked if we could get Jack on the show. It was tough since Jack's tee time was always around noon because CBS wanted Jack on during their prime hours. Unfortunately, this was the same time that we started our show.

One year, however, there was a long rain delay at Pebble Beach. It was such a long delay that all the golfers and celebrities went back to their rooms. They always stayed at The Lodge and most celebrities didn't normally list themselves under their real name. I figured this would be a perfect time to try Jack, but I didn't mention it to Bob or Bruce because I didn't think I had much of a chance to reach him.

I called The Lodge and asked for Jack's room. The hotel operator told me Jack wasn't accepting phone calls to his room. In the radio industry we would say he had a "do not disturb" on his phone. I asked the hotel operator, "Can you please tell him it's Randy with Sporting News Radio?" She said she would call his room and tell him. Unfortunately, I couldn't hear the phone ringing so I couldn't tell what was going on, but maybe thirty seconds later, I heard, "Hello, this is Jack."

I was stunned! I gained my composure and said, "Mr. Lemmon, it's Randy with Sporting News Radio. How are you?"

"Oh, I'm fine Randy. I'm just sitting in my room waiting for the rain to stop."

"Is there any chance you might be willing to do a brief radio interview right now? My hosts are huge fans of yours."

"Sure, no problem. I'm happy to do it."

I was shocked, but I shouldn't have been because he was always so nice. I quickly typed on the screen "go to JACK LEMMON right now!" Bob and Bruce were involved in a discussion and weren't looking at the screen, so I activated the alert button. The look on their faces was priceless. They were psyched!

Jack was great and was willing to answer anything about his movies and Hollywood. At the end of the interview, they thanked him for coming on. He replied, "Okey doke!" I picked up the phone after the interview and thanked him again. He said, "Happy to do it, Randy. Take care now." This was a pretty cool moment. There have not been too many times in my career when I had the opportunity to book a true legend!

Grandpa Munster

Yes, Grandpa Munster. The great actor was also an NBA Scout for the Atlanta Hawks. One-On-One Sports was doing many shows from the Final Four in New York City and back then, in 1996, John Renshaw was our signature show. He was a young, flashy host who knew a ton about sports but was the first host I worked with that also brought in entertainment. He loved reciting lyrics from songs and bringing in pop culture. He had just been moved to afternoons from overnights. On this day, I was sent to the coaches' hotel with the old brick cell phone. My job was to get fun college basketball coaches on the air. The crazy thing is a lot of these coaches listened to Renshaw at night and were huge fans. So, it was easy getting Kelvin Sampson on from Oklahoma, Tubby Smith from Georgia, and others.

I was making my way through the lobby, which is where all the coaches hang out. It takes some time to figure out who is who and there are many out of work coaches looking for a job. I was making my way through the busy lobby when I see, out of the corner of my eye, Grandpa Munster! I thought that he would be a perfect guest for Renshaw.

I called the studio and said, "Ask John if he wants him." I got a quick response, "Absolutely!" I approached Grandpa Munster and explained who I was. He was probably in his 70's by this point. He kind of gave me a look. He was sitting at a table with a drink in his hand and said, "Sure, I'll do it."

"Can I ask you to walk over to the pay phone?"

"F*** no!"

So I handed him the cell phone and reminded him it was live radio.

Renshaw welcomed Grandpa in and, within the first minute, he said "shit" twice. I was freaking out. I'd only been working at One-On-One for two years, so I was thinking, "I'm getting fired." He said it twice more in the next two answers. I ran to the front desk, got a paper and pen, and wrote: "Please stop swearing" and handed it to him. He looked at the note, rolled it up and threw at me. I'm not kidding. He threw it hard! He wrapped up with Renshaw and handed me back the phone and just walked away. He didn't say a word to me. I hung out at the hotel for another hour and got a few more coaches on. I was dreading my walk back to where we were set up because I assumed my boss, Rich Bonn, would give me an earful. It was the exact opposite. They both said, "Great job getting Grandpa. Perfect fit!"

"Weren't you guys pissed about the swearing?"

"Nope. It added to the interview." I breathed a big sigh of relief!

Bill Murray

It was always my dream to book one of my favorite actors, Bill Murray. I grew up on *Stripes* and *Caddyshack*! However, he was a very tough book. Then came Pebble Beach back in the late 90's. There was a rain delay, and the players went back to the lodge for the afternoon, so it was the ideal opportunity for a good producer to strike. I let Bob and Bruce know that I would be trying the hotel in open segments. I had already booked the great Jack Lemmon. Next up was Bill Murray. I couldn't believe he was listed. I asked to ring his room and he answered! I explained I was from a national network in Chicago. He was friendly. I asked if he would come on and he said that he was watching the Bulls! I made my standard plea - I just need him for five minutes. He said, "Sure, go ahead." I put him right up with Bob and Bruce. He was good, but not great. I can tell he was distracted by the game. Sometimes, when you put actors on the radio, it's not always great radio. Anyways, mission accomplished! I booked Bill Murray.

Let's fast forward to 2016 when the Cubs were in the World Series. It was right before game 7. David Kaplan was doing his show from our affiliate in Cleveland. He was getting ready to go to their studios and Bill Murray approached him and started talking about his hotel room and the game that night. Kap asked if he could join his radio show in half an hour. He said he would love to and gave Kap his cell phone. He said to Kap, "Do not give my number to anyone!" Kap said, "No way. I won't give it out." However, I was back in Chicago and Kap had to give me the number to put Bill on the air.

Kap was on at noon and I called Bill on his cell right at noon. He answered but was talking to someone else. Kap was waiting for the thumbs up from our on-sight producer, Adam Abdalla. Finally, Bill said hello. I said, "Bill, it's Randy with Kap. Are you ready to go?"

"Who is this?"

I told him again.

"I told that mother f***** not to give out my cell phone!" Then he hung up.

Kap said on the air, "Randy, do we have Bill?" I jumped on the mic and said, "We are having an issue. Give me a minute." I wasn't done with Bill yet, so I figured why not try him again? I called his cell and he answered again but it was the same situation as the first time. He was talking to someone else. A couple minutes later he finally said hello.

"Bill, it's Randy with Kap. I think we got disconnected. The only reason he gave me your number is so I can put you on the air."

"You again?! Didn't you get the f****** message?" and with that, he hung up again.

Kap was still waiting on the air. I jumped on again.

"Kap, Bill Murray will not be joining us."

At the break, Kap called me and asked what happened. I told him and he was furious. I still don't understand why people act the way. I guess this falls into the category of you win some, you lose some!

Kenny Kramer

Kenny Kramer is the character Michael Richards was based on. I am a huge Seinfeld fan. When I was working at One-On-One Sports, we were going to do our show from Mickey Mantle's restaurant the weekend of the NBA All Star game. I figured it would be a good idea to invite the real Kramer to the show. I reached out to Kenny and he was really excited. He said he would be happy to come by. An hour later, he called me back and said he wanted to know if it was alright if he brought his tour group to the show. I said, "Wait - there actually is a tour bus like Kramer had on Seinfeld?"

"Where do you think he got that from?"

"Great, bring them all. I'm sure Mickey Mantle's can handle it."

Well, he brought a group of twenty people. Kenny came on for two segments and had many great stories. His segments ended and we went on with the show. An hour later, I looked over and he was still there! He came back around and said that if needed, he would be happy to come back on later today or tomorrow. He really was Kramer!

Henry Winkler

Growing up in the 70's and early 80's what kid didn't want to be the Fonz? *Happy Days* was a show that we watched as a family every week. I wanted a leather jacket because of the Fonz. My job in radio has afforded me the opportunity to meet so many amazing people, and in October of 2019, I met the Fonz! I was driving that morning and heard Henry Winkler on another AM station. I thought it would be great to get him in studio, but then I was thinking there is no way Carmen and Jurko would want to talk to him. So I went on with my day. We went down to our State Street Studio to do our show. I want to say around 12:20 pm, right in the middle of a segment, Carmen yelled out, "Merk, did I just see Henry Winkler walk in the building?" I said, "You probably did. He's in town. You want to talk with him?" He said, "Are you kidding me? YES!!"

Henry Winkler was a guest on *Windy City Live*, a local show that airs on ABC from 1-2. At the break, I went to their producer and asked if Henry might have a few minutes to stop by. She said she would check. She came back a couple of minutes later and said she heard he was in a really bad mood and didn't want to do it. I was bummed but understood. Then a few minutes later she came back and said, "Wait, he said he will do it but, he wants to do it in five minutes." I had Adam Schefter booked, but I wasn't going to turn down the Fonz! When I put Schefty on the air, I told him if we cut you short it's because the Fonz might becoming on. He laughed and said that sounded good. A minute later, the producer came back and said he wanted to have makeup done first and then would come by. She emphasized that he was in a bad mood. I communicated to Carmen and Jurko all the details.

I have to admit, I was a little nervous and excited for the opportunity to have Henry Winkler on. Finally around 1:20, the door opened and through that door came the FONZ with some other people behind him. I approached him introduced myself and said, "Mr. Winkler, it's a pleasure to meet you." He said, "It's nice to meet you, Randy, and please call me Henry." He was promoting a new children's book that he wrote, and he had his co-author with him. He introduced me to her as well. I told them both Carmen and Jurko's names and brought them in the studio. Carmen loved Henry Winkler from his work on *Barry*. It's amazing how he transcends culture! I was concerned since I was told that he was in a bad mood, but nothing could be further from the truth. He was outstanding with Carmen and Jurko and was probably on for ten minutes.

After the interview, I asked if he would mind taking a few pictures. He said, "Of course." I did have a second to tell him how the Fonz is one of my favorite characters ever and how I wanted to be him! He was very humble and thanked me. Usually, when you meet one of your childhood idols, you are concerned that they won't live up to the expectations you have set. In this case, Henry Winkler exceeded those expectations and it's a day I will never forget.

Snoop Dogg

It's pretty crazy that I have two Snoop Dogg stories. He is one of the greatest entertainers and a true sports fan. The first one dates back to the Super Bowl in the early 2000's. James Brown was our host from 10am-12pm on Sporting News Radio. He wasn't able to host his show that week because CBS had the Super Bowl. So, Matt Nahigian and Ryan Williams had the bold idea to hire Deion Sanders to host for three days. Deion was different than JB. He wanted a totally different type of guest.

I was producing his show from the studios in Northbrook and Matt would call me every morning before the show with the guest list. On Thursday, he called and said that we were doing Ray Lewis, Jerry Rice and, at 11:30, I would have to call Snoop Dog. I said, "Wait, I'm calling Snoop Dogg?" He said yes and gave me his number. So at 11:29, I called Snoop. Just FYI, I didn't listen to much rap back then. Someone answered the phone and I asked if I could please speak to Snoop Dog. The gentleman asked who it was, and I told him that I was with Deion. He told me to hold on and then Snoop picked up the phone. I said, "Hey Snoop, it's Randy with Deion. Are you ready to go?" He said something indecipherable in return. So I said, "Excuse me?" He said it again and it sounded like "shizzle my dizzle."

"Excuse me?"

"Put me on the air, fool!" So I put him on the air. It was a great interview. After it was done, I said, "Sorry about that, Snoop".

"No problem, my man."

The second time I booked Snoop was in 2019. He was going to be on *Windy City Live*. Danny Zederman was able to convince his people to have him come on *The Carmen and Jurko Show*. He came in with a group of four or five people and everyone was really nice. Snoop was on with Carmen and Jurko for about ten minutes. At the end, Carmen said, "Snoop, thanks so much for coming on." Snoop said, "Are you kidding me? It's great to have the chance to be on ESPN Radio in Chicago. I would never pass that up!"

After he finished, there was a long line from our staff waiting to get a picture with Snoop. Not only did he take a picture with everyone, but he invited us to his suite later that night to partake in some weed smoking! No one took him up on that offer, but it was a very cool moment meeting Snoop.

President Obama

Who wouldn't want to book the President of the United States? It was always my goal to book President Obama while he was in office, but you might ask why. Well, he's an engaging interview and a huge sports fan. Plus, he was a Senator for the great State of Illinois, and he is a diehard Sox and Bulls fan. I knew that in order to book the President, I had to have a hook. I couldn't just reach out to the President's PR staff and ask him to join one of our shows. So, anytime I had a big-name Chicago guest in studio or on the phone for an extended time, I would reach out to the President's PR staff. By the way, getting in touch with the right person to get a request in front of the President took some time to figure out. I finally found the right email and was able to open a line of communication.

My first try was when we did a *Lunch with a Legend* with Scottie Pippen. I reached out to the President's PR staff and I received a quick response, "The President says thank you for the opportunity, but his schedule is too busy." There were a couple of other opportunities, but nothing was getting the President's interest. Finally, I thought I had the right guest. Ozzie Guillen had just taken a job with the Marlins and was leaving in early February to start as their manager. I had set up a *Lunch with a Legend* with Ozzie, so I reached out to the President's PR staff right away and I gave them the particulars of the event. I didn't have high hopes that he would be interested, but a day before the event, I was driving home from work when I received a call on my cell phone. It was strange that my phone was ringing, but nothing was on my screen. It didn't even say "private number." I decided to answer anyways.

The female voice on the other end asked, "Is this Randy Merkin from ESPN 1000?" I told her it was. "This is the President's PR Staff calling. (I can't remember her name.) Your request to join Ozzie Guillen intrigued the President. It's not a yes, but it's certainly not a no. When I presented the opportunity, he didn't right away say no."

She told me to not expect him to call. However, should he call at any time during the one-hour show, he could not be placed on hold and had to go on the air right away. He also would only have two minutes. I was psyched! I didn't have high expectations that he would call in, but the mere fact that he was considering the interview was pretty cool. Unfortunately, the President never called. I tried a few other times with other big-name Chicago guests and once with Charles Barkley in studio, but I was never able to book the President.

Meeting Waddle and Silvy

I spent the first 12 years of my radio career at One-On-One Sports/Sporting News Radio. When they moved their operations to Los Angeles, I decided to stay in Chicago and not go with them. It was the greatest time of my life because my twins, Brett and Dana, were just born and I was able to spend 5 months with my beautiful kids. After many talks with Justin Craig and Adam Delevitt, I accepted a position to become the Executive Producer of the *Waddle and Silvy Show*. I was excited to start the second chapter of my radio career. Justin thought it might be a good idea to have a meeting with the guys before we started. Our meeting was to take place at Salt and Peppa, a restaurant in Wrigleyville, after Waddle and Silvy's remote. It was on a Friday and the Cubs had a 1:20 game. I totally screwed up my timing. I usually parked a mile away to stay clear of the Wrigley crowd. However, with traffic, I didn't park until 11:55. We were meeting at 12:10. I was wearing nice shoes, nice pants and a nice golf shirt, but I started out in a full sprint and didn't stop. Did I mention it was 90 degrees that day? By the time I arrived at Salt and Peppa, I was a sweaty mess!

Of course, Justin picked the only restaurant in Wrigleyville that didn't have air conditioning! I sat down, met the guys, and immediately grabbed about 30 napkins to wipe off my face and under my shirt. Waddle and Silvy were staring at me with a quizzical look. My sweat didn't stop during the whole lunch. I think I had 4 glasses of Ice water within the first twenty minutes. Anyways, we had a good discussion about the show and some other topics. Waddle even asked how we get twins to sleep at the same time!

We got up to leave and I felt the back of my shirt just sticking to me. It was awful. I remember when we left the restaurant, I was walking with Justin and Waddle and Silvy were behind me. I turned around at one point and both of them had a big grin on their face. They were enjoying my discomfort! The worst part is to this day, they still don't let me live this down. I guess you could either get upset or chose to embrace it. I chose to embrace it. It was a great 6 year run with the guys on the *Waddle and Silvy Show*!

ACKNOWLEDGMENTS

Ever since I was a youngster, I knew the career path I wanted to take. I wanted to be in broadcasting. Throughout the years, I have had many people help me in making my dream a reality. It all started at WHFH at Homewood Flossmoor High School, where I worked with the best young broadcasters around. We were all mentored by Robert Comstock, Megan Tipton, and Del Kennedy. They didn't just teach us about radio, but about life as well. Mr. Comstock was my first real mentor, and he was like a second father. What I learned from my time at WHFH, I still apply to what I do today.

Before I landed my first radio job, I had a chance to intern at WGN Radio. Chuck Swirsky, Wayne Larrivee, Randy Minkoff and Thom Brennamen gave me the freedom to learn on the job and taught me a ton. I also would like to thank Brett Dolan and Michelle Eccles who helped me survive my first radio job in Platteville. That's a whole different book!

I was fortunate to land at a great company for a young broadcaster, One-On-One Sports. This is where I really learned I could be successful at my job. I worked with great people who taught me all about the industry, including Mark Gentzkow, Steve Czaban, Papa Joe Chevalier and Larry Cotlar. I was lucky enough to work side by side with three of the best in the industry, Matt Nahigian, Rob Wuczynski and Craig Larson. They raised my game every day. For seven years I produced for outstanding hosts every weekend. It started with Bob Berger and Bruce Murray and ended with Bob Berger and Bob Stelton. Those are three of the greatest people you would ever want to work with, and I had the time of my life.

My job for the last 13 years has been at ESPN 1000. I was lucky enough to be brought in by the great Justin Craig and Adam Delevitt. The first six years I was Waddle and Silvy's producer. What an amazing ride! They gave me full liberty to spread my wings and book the unobtainable guest. I treasure the friendship and professional relationship I have built with both guys. During my time with Waddle & Silvy, and through today, they developed relationships with some of the biggest names in sports, including Charles Barkley, Al Michaels and Tony Dungy.

    I also have been fortunate enough to work with Carmen, Jurko and Kap. While every relationship is different, I have learned so much from working with all three of these men. I would be remiss to not thank some of the great producers I have worked with at ESPN, including Danny Zederman, Bill Ociepka, Billy Zurekat, Jeff Meller, Adam Abdalla and Chris Bleck. Lastly, a big shout out to the main bosses who always had my back- Chris Brennan, Jim Pastor and Mike Thomas. Thank you.

    Writing this book has been a challenging yet rewarding process. Through it all, my wife Beth has been my rock. From reading drafts and wordsmithing to giving me advice on all aspects of this book, I could not have done it without her support.

ABOUT THE AUTHOR

Randy Merkin has been a Sports Radio Producer for 27 years. He worked for the national sports radio network One-On-One Sports, which became Sporting News Radio. He is currently the Operations Manager and Executive Producer for ESPN 1000. Randy lives in the Chicagoland Area with his wife and teenage twins. *Behind the Glass: Stories from a Sports Radio Producer* is Randy's first book. You can follow him on Twitter at @randymerkin

Photo Credit:
Susan Ryan Kalina
Photography